Spectrum Test Prep

Grade 6
Revised Edition

Test Preparation for:

Reading
Language
Math

Program Authors:
Dale Foreman
Alan C. Cohen
Jerome D. Kaplan
Ruth Mitchell

Send all inquiries to:
McGraw-Hill Consumer Products
250 Old Wilson Bridge Road
Worthington, Ohio 43085

1-57768-106-1

4 5 6 7 8 9 01 02 00 99

Table of Contents

Spectrum Test Prep
The Program That Teaches Test-Taking Achievement

For over two decades, McGraw-Hill has helped students perform their best when taking standardized achievement tests. Over the years, we have identified the skills and strategies that students need to master the challenges of taking a standardized test. Becoming familiar with the test-taking experience can help ensure your child's success.

Spectrum Test Prep covers all test skill areas

Spectrum Test Prep contains the subject areas that are represented in the five major standardized tests. *Spectrum Test Prep* will help your child prepare for the following tests:

- California Achievement Tests® (CAT/5)
- Comprehensive Tests of Basic Skills (CTBS/4)
- Iowa Tests of Basic Skills® (ITBS, Form K)
- Metropolitan Achievement Test (MAT/7)
- Stanford Achievement Test(SAT/9)

Spectrum Test Prep provides strategies for success

Many students need special support when preparing to take a standardized test. *Spectrum Test Prep* gives your child the opportunity to practice and become familiar with:

- General test content
- The test format
- Listening and following standard directions
- Working in structured settings
- Maintaining a silent, sustained effort
- Using test-taking strategies

Spectrum Test Prep is comprehensive

Spectrum Test Prep provides a complete presentation of the types of skills covered in standardized tests in a variety of formats. These formats are similar to those your child will encounter when testing. The subject areas covered in this book include:

- Reading
- Language
- Math

Spectrum Test Prep gives students the practice they need

Each student lesson provides several components that help develop test-taking skills:

- An **Example,** with directions and sample test items
- A **Tips** feature, that gives test-taking strategies
- A **Practice** section, to help students practice answering questions in each test format

Each book gives focused test practice that builds confidence:

- A **Test Yourself** lesson for each unit gives students the opportunity to apply what they have learned in the unit
- A **Test Practice** section gives students the experience of a longer test-like situation.
- A **Progress Chart** allows students to note and record their own progress.

Spectrum Test Prep is the first and most successful program ever developed to help students become familiar with the test-taking experience. *Spectrum Test Prep* can help to build self-confidence, reduce test anxiety, and provide the opportunity for students to successfully show what they have learned.

A Message to Parents and Teachers:

- **Standardized tests: the yardstick for your child's future**

  Standardized testing is one of the cornerstones of American education. From its beginning in the early part of this century, standardized testing has gradually become the yardstick by which student performance is judged. For better or worse, your child's future will be determined in great part by how well she or he performs on the standardized test used by your school district.

- **Even good students can have trouble with testing**

  In general, standardized tests are well designed and carefully developed to assess students' abilities in a consistent and balanced manner. However, there are many factors that can hinder the performance of an individual student when testing. These might include test anxiety, unfamiliarity with the test's format, or failing to understand the directions.

  In addition, it is rare that students are taught all of the material that appears on a standardized test. This is because the curriculum of most schools does not directly match the content of the standardized test. There will certainly be overlap between what your child learns in school and how he or she is tested, but some materials will probably be unfamiliar.

- **Ready to Test will lend a helping hand**

  It is because of the shortcomings of the standardized testing process that *Spectrum Test Prep* was developed. The lessons in the book were created after a careful analysis of the most popular achievement tests. The items, while different from those on the tests, reflect the types of material that your child will encounter when testing. Students who use *Spectrum Test Prep* will also become familiar with the format of the most popular achievement tests. This learning experience will reduce anxiety and give your child the opportunity to do his or her best on the next standardized test.

We urge you to review with your child the Message to Students and the feature "How to Use This Book" on pages 8-9. The information on these pages will help your child to use this book and develop important test-taking skills. We are confident that following the recommendations in this book will help your child to earn a test score that accurately reflects his or her true ability.

A Message to Students:

Frequently in school you will be asked to take a standardized achievement test. This test will show how much you know compared to other students in your grade. Your score on a standardized achievement test will help your teachers plan your education. It will also give you and your parents an idea of what your learning strengths and weaknesses are.

This book will help you do your best on a standardized achievement test. It will show you what to expect on the test and will give you a chance to practice important reading and test-taking skills. Here are some suggestions you can follow to make the best use of *Spectrum Test Prep*.

Plan for success

- You'll do your best if you begin studying and do one or two lessons in this book each week. If you only have a little bit of time before a test is given, you can do one or two lessons each day.
- Study a little bit at a time, no more than 30 minutes a day. If you can, choose the same time each day to study in a quiet place.
- Keep a record of your score on each lesson. The charts on pp. 155 - 157 of this book will help you do this.

On the day of the test . . .

- Get a good night's sleep the night before the test. Have a light breakfast and lunch to keep from feeling drowsy during the test.
- Use the tips you learned in *Spectrum Test Prep*. The most important tips are to skip difficult items, take the best guess when you're unsure of the answer, and try all the items.
- Don't worry if you are a little nervous when you take an achievement test. This is a natural feeling and may even help you stay alert.

How to Use This Book

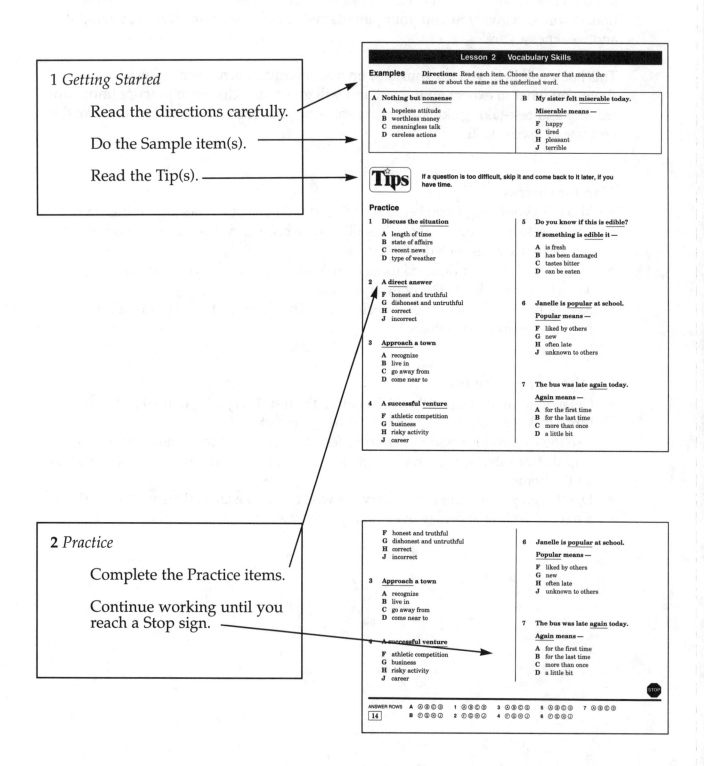

1 *Getting Started*

Read the directions carefully.

Do the Sample item(s).

Read the Tip(s).

2 *Practice*

Complete the Practice items.

Continue working until you reach a Stop sign.

Lesson 2   Vocabulary Skills

Examples   **Directions:** Read each item. Choose the answer that means the same or about the same as the underlined word.

A Nothing but <u>nonsense</u>

   A hopeless attitude
   B worthless money
   C meaningless talk
   D careless actions

B My sister felt <u>miserable</u> today.

   <u>Miserable means</u> —

   F happy
   G tired
   H pleasant
   J terrible

Tips   If a question is too difficult, skip it and come back to it later, if you have time.

Practice

1 Discuss the <u>situation</u>

   A length of time
   B state of affairs
   C recent news
   D type of weather

2 A <u>direct</u> answer

   F honest and truthful
   G dishonest and untruthful
   H correct
   J incorrect

3 <u>Approach</u> a town

   A recognize
   B live in
   C go away from
   D come near to

4 A successful <u>venture</u>

   F athletic competition
   G business
   H risky activity
   J career

5 Do you know if this is <u>edible</u>?

   If something is <u>edible</u> it —

   A is fresh
   B has been damaged
   C tastes bitter
   D can be eaten

6 Janelle is <u>popular</u> at school.

   <u>Popular means</u> —

   F liked by others
   G new
   H often late
   J unknown to others

7 The bus was late <u>again</u> today.

   <u>Again means</u> —

   A for the first time
   B for the last time
   C more than once
   D a little bit

   F honest and truthful
   G dishonest and untruthful
   H correct
   J incorrect

3 <u>Approach</u> a town

   A recognize
   B live in
   C go away from
   D come near to

4 A successful <u>venture</u>

   F athletic competition
   G business
   H risky activity
   J career

6 Janelle is <u>popular</u> at school.

   <u>Popular means</u> —

   F liked by others
   G new
   H often late
   J unknown to others

7 The bus was late <u>again</u> today.

   <u>Again means</u> —

   A for the first time
   B for the last time
   C more than once
   D a little bit

STOP

ANSWER ROWS   **A** ⒶⒷⒸⒹ   **1** ⒶⒷⒸⒹ   **3** ⒶⒷⒸⒹ   **5** ⒶⒷⒸⒹ   **7** ⒶⒷⒸⒹ
14   **B** ⒻⒼⒽⒿ   **2** ⒻⒼⒽⒿ   **4** ⒻⒼⒽⒿ   **6** ⒻⒼⒽⒿ

3 Check It Out

Check your answers by turning to the Answer Key at the back of the book.

Keep track of how you're doing by marking the number right on the Progress Charts on pages 155-157.

Mark the lesson you completed on the table of contents for each section.

Answer Keys

page 150

Answer Keys		1	C	31	D	16	G
		2	G	32	J	17	D
Reading		3	D	33	C	18	F
Unit 1,		4	F	34	F	19	C
Vocabulary		5	D	35	B	20	J
Lesson 1		6	G	Unit 2, Reading		21	B
A	D	Lesson 6		Comprehension		Lesson 11
B	F	A	C	Lesson 8		A	B
1	C	B	G	A	D	1	D
2	J	1	D	1	C	2	G
3	A	2	H	2	F	3	C
4	F	3	A	3	D	4	F
5	A	4	H	4	G	5	A
6	H	5	B	Lesson 9		6	H
7	D	6	A	1	D	7	B
8	G	Lesson 7		2	H	8	H
Lesson 2		E1	D	3	C	9	D
A	C	E2	F	4	F	10	J
B	J	1	C	5	B	11	A
1	B	2	F	6	J	12	H
2	F	3	D	7	B	13	B
3	D	4	H	8	H	14	F
4	G	5	D	9	D	15	J
5	D	6	G	10	H	16	J
6	F	7	A	11	A	17	C
7	C	8	H	12	G	18	G
Lesson 3		9	D	13	B	19	A
A	C	10	F	14	H	20	F
B	G	11	B	15	A	21	D
1	C	12	H	16	J	22	J
2	G	13	D	Lesson 10		23	D
3	D	14	J	A	C	24	F
4	C	15	C	1	A	25	C
5	B	16	G	2	F	26	A
6	J	17	D	3	D	27	A
7	A	18	F	4	H	28	G
8	J	19	A	5	D	29	B
Lesson 4		20	H	6	F	30	J
A	C	21	B	7	B	Unit 3, Test
B	G	22	F	8	H	Practice
1	D	23	C	9	A	Part 1
2	F	24	F	10	J	E1	C
3	A	25	C	11	C	E2	J
4	J	26	H	12	F	1	B
5	D	27	A	13	C	2	J
Lesson 5		28	H	14	F	3	D
A	A	29	H	15	B	4	G
B	J	30	G			5	D

Reading Progress Chart

Circle your score for each lesson. Connect your scores to see how well you are doing.

page 155

Unit 1 Lesson 1	Lesson 2	Lesson 3	Lesson 4	Lesson 5	Lesson 6	Lesson 7	Unit 2 Lesson 8	Lesson 9	Lesson 10	Lesson 11
8	7	8	5	6	6	35 34 33 32 31 30 29 28 27 26 25 24 23 22 21 20 19 18 17 16 15 14 13 12 11 10 9 8 7 6 5 4 3 2 1	4	16 15 14 13 12 11 10 9 8 7 6 5 4 3 2	21 20 19 18 17 16 15 14 13 12 11 10 9 8 7 6 5 4 3 2 1	30 29 28 27 26 25 24 23 22 21 20 19 18 17 16 15 14 13 12 11 10 9 8 7 6 5 4 3 2 1
7	6	7	4	5	5		3			
6	5	6								
5	4	5	3	4	4		2			
4	3	4		3	3					
3		3	2							
2	2	2		2	2					
1	1	1	1	1	1		1			

Table of Contents
Reading

page 12

Skills

Reading

VOCABULARY

Identifying synonyms
Identifying words with similar meanings
Identifying word meaning from a derivational clue
Identifying antonyms

Identifying multi-meaning words
Identifying words from a defining statement
Identifying words in paragraph context
Identifying affix meaning

READING COMPREHENSION

Recognizing story structures
Differentiating between fact and opinion
Making comparisons
Identifying story genres
Recognizing details
Using a story web
Understanding events
Drawing conclusions
Applying story information
Deriving word or phrase meaning
Understanding characters
Identifying relevant reference sources

Sequencing ideas
Making inferences
Predicting outcomes
Generalizing from story information
Predicting from story content
Identifying reading strategies
Choosing the best title for a passage
Extending a story's meaning
Understanding the author's purpose
Understanding feelings
Understanding the main idea
Understanding literary devices

Language Arts

LANGUAGE MECHANICS

Identifying the need for punctuation marks
(period, question mark, exclamation
point, quotation marks, apostrophe,
comma) in sentences

Identifying the need for capital letters and
punctuation marks in printed text

LANGUAGE EXPRESSION

Identifying the correct forms of verbs,
adjectives, and pronouns
Identifying the predicate of a sentence
Identifying correctly formed sentences
Identifying sentences that do not fit in a paragraph
Combining sentences

Choosing the right paragraph for a given
purpose
Identifying the subject of a sentence
Identifying the correct sentence to
complete a paragraph
Recognizing double negatives

SPELLING

Identifying correctly spelled words

Identifying incorrectly spelled words

STUDY SKILLS

Understanding an outline web
Using a telephone directory
Understanding a catalog card
Understanding an encyclopedia
or dictionary

Using an index or table of contents
Alphabetizing words
Identifying reference sources
Identifying organizational method
Using a reference table

Math

CONCEPTS

Associating numerals and number words

Comparing and ordering fractions and decimals

Comparing and ordering whole numbers, integers, and Roman numerals
Factoring numbers and finding the greatest common factor
Identifying fractional parts
Recognizing equivalent fractions
Recognizing odd and even numbers
Reducing fractions
Renaming fractions
Understanding decimal place value
Understanding number sentences
Using a number line with fractions and decimals
Using operational symbols and properties

Converting between decimals and fractions
Estimating
Finding multiples
Finding square roots
Identifying the lowest common denominator
Recognizing numeric patterns
Recognizing prime and composite numbers
Regrouping
Rounding
Understanding function tables
Understanding place value
Using expanded notation

COMPUTATION

Adding whole numbers, decimals, and fractions
Subtracting whole numbers, decimals, and fractions

Dividing whole numbers, decimals, and fractions
Multiplying whole numbers, decimals, and fractions

APPLICATIONS

Estimating weight and size
Formulating simple number sentences
Reading a thermometer
Recognizing plane and solid figures and their characteristics
Solving word problems
Understanding bar, line, and circle graphs
Understanding inequalities
Understanding probability, averages, and combinations
Using tables and charts
Using standard and metric units of measurement

Finding perimeter, area, and volume
Identifying information needed to solve a problem
Recognizing value of money and money notation
Solving simple equations
Understanding congruence and transformations
Understanding points, lines, segments, and angles, and their characteristics
Understanding ratio and proportion
Understanding time concepts
Using a coordinate graph

Strategies

Listening carefully
Following group directions
Utilizing test formats
Locating questions and answer choices
Following oral directions
Subvocalizing answer choices
Working methodically
Skipping difficult items and returning to them later
Identifying and using key words to find the answer
Staying with the first answer choice
Recalling the meaning of familiar words
Trying out answer choices
Eliminating answer choices
Checking answer choices
Skimming a passage
Using logic
Indicating that an item has no mistakes
Checking answers by the opposite operation
Converting problems to a workable format
Noting the lettering of answer choices
Taking the best guess when unsure of the answer
Indicating that the correct answer is not given
Identifying the best test-taking strategy
Following written directions
Evaluating answer choices
Recalling the elements of a correctly formed sentence
Referring to a passage to find the correct answer

Marking the correct answer as soon as it is found
Adjusting to a structured setting
Maintaining a silent, sustained effort
Managing time effectively
Considering every answer choice
Computing carefully
Ignoring extraneous information
Using context to find the answer
Locating the correct answer
Understanding unusual item formats
Following complex directions
Responding to items according to difficulty
Reasoning from facts and evidence
Referring to a passage to answer questions
Following complex directions
Avoiding over-analysis of answer choices
Referring to a reference source
Restating a question
Finding the answer without computing
Performing the correct operation
Previewing items
Identifying and using key words, figures, and numbers
Comparing answer choices
Reworking a problem
Recalling the elements of a correctly formed paragraph

Table of Contents
Reading

UNIT 1   VOCABULARY

Lesson 1   Synonyms

Examples   Directions: Read each item. Choose the word that means the same or about the same as the underlined word.

A a long **conflict**	B An **abrupt** stop is —
A friendship	F sudden
B time	G slow
C project	H planned
D struggle	J difficult

Look carefully at all the answer choices.

When you mark your answer, be sure you are marking it in the right space in the answer rows.

Practice

1   carefully select

A eliminate
B measure
C choose
D align

2   circulate a rumor

F ignore
G hear
H trust
J spread

3   deeply eroded

A worn
B steep
C high
D rugged

4   pardon someone

F forgive
G slide
H pause
J compete

5   To irritate people is to —

A annoy
B chase
C enjoy
D visit

6   A forceful person is —

F weak
G foreign
H strong
J helpful

7   An insistent salesperson is —

A talented
B capable
C friendly
D persistent

8   A significant discovery is —

F profitable
G important
H unexpected
J surprising

STOP

Examples   **Directions:** Read each item. Choose the answer that means the same or about the same as the underlined word.

A Nothing but nonsense	**B My sister felt miserable today.**
(A) hopeless attitude	**Miserable means —**
B worthless money	**F** happy
C meaningless talk	**G** tired
D careless actions	**H** pleasant
	(J) terrible

 If a question is too difficult, skip it and come back to it later, if you have time.

Practice

1 Discuss the situation

    A length of time
    B state of affairs
    C recent news
    D type of weather

2 A direct answer

    F honest and truthful
    G dishonest and untruthful
    H correct
    J incorrect

3 Approach a town

    A recognize
    B live in
    C go away from
    D come near to

4 A successful venture

    F athletic competition
    G business
    H risky activity
    J career

5 Do you know if this is edible?

    If something is edible it —

    A is fresh
    B has been damaged
    C tastes bitter
    D can be eaten

6 Janelle is popular at school.

    Popular means —

    F liked by others
    G new
    H often late
    J unknown to others

7 The bus was late again today.

    Again means —

    A for the first time
    B for the last time
    C more than once
    D a little bit

STOP

Examples   **Directions:** Read each item. Choose the answer that means the opposite of the underlined word.

A will <u>decline</u>	B <u>peddle</u> newspapers
A decrease	F read
B enlist	G buy
C increase	H sell
D pause	J order

If you are not sure which answer is correct, take your best guess.

Eliminate answers that mean the same as the underlined word.

Practice

1   be <u>lenient</u>

A   easy
B   complex
C   strict
D   written

2   <u>nourish</u> plants

F   starve
G   cultivate
H   harvest
J   rescue

3   <u>rare</u> disease

A   unusual
B   severe
C   mild
D   common

4   try to <u>surrender</u>

F   follow
G   resist
H   arrest
J   delete

5   <u>migrate</u> with many others

A   move
B   remain
C   disagree
D   build

6   <u>blunt</u> answer

F   correct
G   difficult
H   long and detailed
J   short and rude

7   <u>ordinary</u> people

A   unusual
B   normal
C   kind
D   surprising

8   feel <u>relieved</u>

F   satisfied
G   without worry
H   angry about
J   concerned

Examples   Directions: Read the directions carefully. For items A and 1-2, choose the answer you think is correct. For items B and 3-5, choose the word that fits in both sentences.

A | Part of this puzzle is missing. |

In which sentence does the word part mean the same thing as in the sentence above?

A   On which side do you part your hair?

B   Marcello has a small part in the play.

C   This is an important part of the engine.

D   Mix one part of juice to three of water.

B   You can _____ the flowers there.

Is this the right _____ ?

F   put

G   place

H   location

J   arrange

Use the meaning of the sentences to find the right answer.

Check your answer one last time before you mark the circle.

Practice

1 | This column of numbers is wrong. |

In which sentence does the word column mean the same thing as in the sentence above?

A   The column of soldiers marched by.

B   A large column held up the roof.

C   Janna's newspaper column was funny.

D   The research results were arranged in a single column.

2 | This river begins as a small spring. |

In which sentence does the word spring mean the same thing as in the sentence above?

F   We found a cool spring beside the trail.

G   The lid was held shut by a spring.

H   The rescue workers can spring into action quickly.

J   A mountain goat will often spring from rock to rock.

3   My aunt was recently promoted to the rank of _____ in the U.S. Air Force.

I know the _____ area near camp.

A   general

B   major

C   immediate

D   approximate

4   The plane will _____ between five and six o'clock tonight.

How much _____ do you own?

F   arrive

G   property

H   come

J   land

5   You can earn _____ on your money.

Her greatest _____ is African art.

A   profits

B   enjoyment

C   payment

D   interest

STOP

Examples   **Directions:** Read the paragraph. Find the word below the paragraph that fits best in each numbered blank.

The ___(A)___ of our new house is beside a lake. Several other houses are nearby, but they are ___(B)___ by tall trees. The families who live near the lake have the right to use it for swimming and boating.

A   A   site
    B   mortgage
    C   approach
    D   door

B   F   populated
    G   aligned
    H   censored
    J   concealed

If you aren't sure which answer is correct, substitute each answer in the blank.

Practice

The legal system that governs our actions today is ___(1)___ from several ___(2)___ . Much of our legal system comes from English common law. This body of law was ___(3)___ created by the kings that ruled after 1100 A.D. Another contribution from England was the *Magna Carta*, a ___(4)___ that stated that everyone, including the king himself, was subject to the law. The most ___(5)___ source of our legal system is the Constitution. It ___(6)___ everything from the branches of government to the age required to run for President.

1   A   attached
    B   situated
    C   derived
    D   serviced

4   F   document
    G   motion
    H   fiction
    J   sponsor

2   F   topics
    G   sources
    H   regions
    J   possibilities

5   A   realistic
    B   ferocious
    C   needless
    D   noteworthy

3   A   finally
    B   recently
    C   hopefully
    D   initially

6   F   blames
    G   specifies
    H   offends
    J   detects

STOP

Examples   **Directions:** Read each question. Fill in the circle for the answer you think is correct.

A Which of these words probably comes from the Latin word *manus* meaning *hand*?

- **A** minimize
- **B** measurable
- **C** manage
- **D** motion

B Businesses now _____ important papers before throwing them away.

Which of these words would indicate that the papers were cut into pieces?

- **F** bolt
- **G** shred
- **H** slam
- **J** fix

Stay with your first answer. It is right more often than it is wrong.

Practice

1 Which of these words probably comes from the French word *étage* meaning *a place to stand*?

- **A** eaten
- **B** attempt
- **C** stranger
- **D** stage

2 Which of these words probably comes from the Italian word *corriere* meaning *to run*?

- **F** control
- **G** court
- **H** courier
- **J** count

---

3 The family of the injured child found the newspaper reports _____ .

Which of these words means the family did not like the reports?

- **A** offensive
- **B** insatiable
- **C** enlightened
- **D** customary

4 The _____ was almost empty.

Which of these words would indicate that the food closet was almost empty?

- **F** oven
- **G** trunk
- **H** pantry
- **J** purse

For numbers 5 and 6, choose the answer that best defines the underlined part.

5 fish<u>ery</u>   print<u>ery</u>

- **A** time when
- **B** place where
- **C** with
- **D** almost

6 <u>aqua</u>rium   <u>aqua</u>tic

- **F** pertaining to water
- **G** pertaining to air
- **H** without fear
- **J** without speed

STOP

ANSWER ROWS   **A** Ⓐ Ⓑ Ⓒ Ⓓ   **1** Ⓐ Ⓑ Ⓒ Ⓓ   **3** Ⓐ Ⓑ Ⓒ Ⓓ   **5** Ⓐ Ⓑ Ⓒ Ⓓ

18   **B** Ⓕ Ⓖ Ⓗ Ⓙ   **2** Ⓕ Ⓖ Ⓗ Ⓙ   **4** Ⓕ Ⓖ Ⓗ Ⓙ   **6** Ⓕ Ⓖ Ⓗ Ⓙ

Examples   Directions: For items E1 and 1-8, find the word or words that mean the same or almost the same as the underlined word. For item E-2, mark the answer you think is correct.

E1 similar clothes

   A different
   B expensive
   C dull
   D alike

E2 Which of these probably comes from the Old French word *trenchier* meaning *to cut*?

   F trench
   G triangle
   H traffic
   J intricate

---

1 large structure

   A mountain
   B window
   C building
   D vehicle

5 A person who is eager —

   A is exhausted
   B came late for something
   C missed an opportunity
   D is enthusiastic

2 unusual weather

   F abnormal
   G unpleasant
   H normal
   J good

6 To dispense is to —

   F come out
   G give out
   H throw away
   J save money for

3 delay her trip

   A enjoy
   B afford
   C hasten
   D postpone

7 Prior means —

   A coming before
   B waiting beside
   C following closely
   D in place of

4 be cautious

   F reckless
   G calm
   H careful
   J happy

8 If something is humorous it is —

   F obvious
   G subtle
   H funny
   J boring

GO

9 Andy was <u>injured</u> in the baseball game.

To be <u>injured</u> is to be —

A good
B excited
C tired
D hurt

10 The South American hunter carried his <u>spear</u> proudly.

A <u>spear</u> is a —

F weapon
G hat
H prize
J shield

11 The deer seemed to <u>vanish</u> into the woods.

To <u>vanish</u> is to —

A jump
B disappear
C walk
D emerge

12 In the box was a <u>delicate</u> piece of glass.

If something is <u>delicate</u> it is —

F beautiful
G very expensive
H easily broken
J sturdy

13 She has a <u>temporary</u> job as a cook.

<u>Temporary</u> means —

A for a long time
B difficult
C relaxing
D for a short time

For numbers 14-19, find the word that means the opposite of the underlined word.

14 brief <u>pause</u>

F journey
G break
H inspection
J continuation

15 will <u>accumulate</u>

A evaluate
B suspend
C distribute
D stockpile

16 <u>corrupt</u> person

F comical
G honest
H competitive
J crooked

17 known <u>formerly</u>

A before
B widely
C personally
D currently

18 <u>slender</u> branch

F thick
G thin
H strong
J weak

19 <u>vital</u> mission

A unimportant
B essential
C strong
D irate

GO

For numbers 20-23, choose the word that correctly completes both sentences.

20 We need a new _____ in the kitchen.

The _____ of scores was 70 to 100.

F oven
G span
H range
J table

21 The woods are _____ here.

The ice was not very_____ .

A pretty
B thick
C hard
D dark

22 The _____ house is ours.

In a _____, the bird was gone.

F second
G last
H minute
J small

23 We should _____ this tire now.

A _____ of flowers was near the door.

A fix
B bunch
C patch
D replace

24 | If you park there, you will block the driveway. |

In which sentence does the word block mean the same thing as in the sentence above?

F You can block the door with this brick.
G Our block has some great trees.
H Jean's brother carved this block of wood into the shape of a cat.
J We bought a block of tickets to the game.

25 | State your name and address. |

In which sentence does the word state mean the same thing as in the sentence above?

A Each state has its own capital.
B Her state of mind was positive when she started the race.
C When you state your position, speak clearly.
D The old farmhouse was in a poor state.

For numbers 26 and 27, choose the answer that best defines the underlined part.

26 displace   discharge

F not
G almost
H away from
J in the direction of

27 civilize   crystallize

A to become
B to weaken
C very much
D instead of

GO

28 Which of these words probably comes from the Latin word *tolerare* meaning *to bear pain*?

F tool
G total
H tolerate
J torture

29 Which of these words probably comes from the Old English word *bindan* meaning *to tie*?

A bind
B band
C bend
D blind

30 The _____ for animals is often improved by sensible development.

Which of these words means the place where animals live?

F garment
G habitat
H tropical
J treasury

31 An _____ bystander identified the criminal.

Which of these words means the person paid attention to what he or she saw?

A splendid
B fidgety
C instinctive
D observant

Read the paragraph. Find the word below the paragraph that fits best in each numbered blank.

Manufacturing has changed ___(32)___ in the last hundred years. Around the turn of the ___(33)___ , manufacturing required much hand labor. When machines were used, they were powered by steam or water. Today, much less human labor is required because ___(34)___ machines do so much of the work. Most contemporary manufacturing equipment is powered by electricity, and you rarely see the ___(35)___ of steam that signaled a nineteenth-century factory.

32 F little
G confusingly
H hastily
J considerably

33 A decade
B time
C century
D age

34 F precision
G ominous
H overgrown
J recognition

35 A plateaus
B plumes
C trifles
D wads

STOP

Lesson 8   Critical Reading

Example

Directions: Read each item. Choose the answer you think is correct. Mark the space for your answer.

Near the beach, secluded among the sand dunes, was a small freshwater pond. It was fed by a spring and remained cool even during the hottest summer days. The plants and animals that made their homes around the spring were unusual for this part of the state.	**A** **What part of a story does this passage tell about?** **A** the plot **B** the characters **C** the mood **D** the setting

If a question sounds confusing, try to restate it to yourself in simpler terms. Be sure you understand the question before you choose an answer.

Practice

1   **Which of these probably came from a geography book?**

A During Jefferson's presidency, America greatly expanded its borders.

B Dirt is primarily composed of clay, silt, and sand.

C Natural features often form the border between countries.

D The principles that keep a plane aloft are easy to understand.

2   **Kim is reading a story about a woman pioneer in the American West after the Civil War. Which of these is most likely to be the beginning of the story?**

F Susan kissed her parents good-bye and boarded the train.

G When she arrived in Deadwood, Susan was amazed at what she saw.

H This was Susan's tenth year in the mountains.

J The friends she had made among the ranchers supported Susan's ideas.

3   Washington, DC, has everything for the visitor, from famous monuments and museums to boating on the Potomac.

A passage like this would most likely be found in a —

A fable.

B biography.

C history book.

D traveler's guide.

4   **Which of these descriptions of a festival states an opinion?**

F This is the twentieth year the festival has been held.

G This year's festival is the best ever.

H More people attended the festival this year than ever before.

J The festival was held in the town park.

STOP

Example

Directions: Read the passage. Find the best answer to each question that follows the passage.

Gardeners around the country are discovering the virtues of grass. Not the kind you mow, but large, decorative grasses that are close cousins of the sprouts in the typical lawn. Ornamental grasses have a number of advantages: they require little water, deer don't eat them, they grow quickly, and they come in a number of beautiful varieties.

A **Which of these is an advantage of ornamental grasses?**

  A Quick growth

  B Eaten by deer

  C Beautiful flowers

  D Grow in moist soil

Look for key words in the question, then find the same words in the passage. This will help you locate the correct answer.

Practice

Here is a story about a girl's feeling when she first encountered a mountain lion. Read the story and then do numbers 1 through 8 on page 25.

When we moved to a small town a few hours from Denver, I didn't think much about it. We had lived in small towns before, and I kind of liked them. It wasn't as exciting as living in the city or the suburbs, but it wasn't bad. The kids were great, and I enjoyed doing lots of things outdoors.

A few weeks after we moved into our house, I heard a terrible sound around sundown that froze my blood. It sounded like an animal screaming. My mother said it was probably a mountain lion, and my heart almost stopped. A mountain lion was close enough to our house for me to hear it. I was terrified.

The next day in school, I asked some of my friends about it. They said there were a few mountain lions in the area, but they didn't bother anyone. Occasionally, a lion would kill a calf or sheep on a farm, but they pretty much stayed away from the town and the houses around it. None of them had ever seen a mountain lion, but all of them had heard one.

I heard the lion again often, but never saw it...that is, until I was hiking with my family a few months later. We had gotten an early start and were heading up a trail beside a canyon. My father told us to stop and be quiet. He pointed across the canyon and there it was. The lion was lying on a ledge, enjoying the warmth of the first rays of the sun. It looked almost like a house cat finding a sunny spot on the floor.

We watched the great cat for a few minutes and then began walking up the trail. As soon as we started moving, the lion jumped up and stared at us. For a few seconds he looked right at me, and I was surprised that I felt no fear. It was almost as if the cat understood that I posed no threat, that I was just another creature in the mountains. Then, with a few great leaps, the cat disappeared over a ridge.

I never saw the big cat again. It's a funny thing, though. I began thinking of the mountain lion as mine, and whenever I heard it calling in the night, I was sure it was letting me know it was all right.

GO

1 According to the story, which of these is true about the narrator?

A She prefers small towns to cities.

B She dislikes cities.

C She dislikes small towns.

D She prefers cities to small towns.

2 How did the narrator feel about the mountain lion at the end of the story?

F Frightened

G Indifferent

H Possessive

J Abandoned

3 Which of these would be most likely to dislike a mountain lion?

A A hiker

B A store owner

C A farmer

D A student

4 In the story, the phrase "froze my blood" means —

F the narrator was frightened.

G the narrator was cold.

H the father was angry.

J the mother was alarmed.

5 The narrator in this story —

A saw the mountain lion before hearing it.

B heard the mountain lion before seeing it.

C followed the mountain lion.

D became concerned about farm animals.

6 The mountain lion is compared to a —

F hunting wolf.

G dog curled up on a pillow.

H snake ready to strike.

J cat in a sunny spot.

7 Which of these statements about mountain lions is true, according to the story?

A Mountain lions are only found in the mountains.

B Mountain lions generally avoid people.

C Mountain lions occasionally "adopt" human families.

D Mountain lions prefer cold weather.

8 The narrator learned about mountain lions from —

F her mother.

G her father.

H friends at school.

J a library book.

GO

As part of a pen pal project, Ashihiro kept a journal of what the weather was like on the first day of every month for his friend in Argentina. Use the journal to do numbers 9-16.

January 1   The ground is covered with about an inch of snow. It is very cold, about 10°, but the sun is shining and the sky is perfectly blue. The wind is blowing at about ten miles an hour from the west. Clouds are supposed to start moving in this afternoon.

February 1   I can't believe how warm it is, almost 40°. There are a few clouds, but it is mostly sunny. The high today is going to be almost 60°. This warm weather is something we call the "January thaw," but this year it happened in February instead.

March 1   This is probably the most miserable day of the year. It's raining, cloudy, and the wind is blowing. I'm glad it's Saturday. Whenever we have weather like this on the weekend my computer gets a good workout.

April 1   It snowed almost 10 inches last night! Only kidding…it's an April Fool's Day joke. Today is beautiful, and my friends and I are going to the park to play baseball. I play the outfield and am pretty good, but not as good as my older sister.

May 1   The wind is really blowing and a storm is coming in. The weather report says we might have thunder and lightning for the first time this year. I love storms, as long as I can be inside.

June 1   School will be over in two more weeks! I hope the weather all summer is like this. The temperature is supposed to be 70° and there isn't a cloud in the sky. I'll be staring out the window in school all day.

July 1   What a dreadful day! The temperature is already 80°, it's damp and sticky, and there isn't a breeze anywhere. I wish we had a swimming pool, but living in the city in an apartment makes that impossible.

August 1   The weather has finally started to cool off. All of July was humid, almost exactly like the day I wrote you. It was impossible to sleep at night because it was so sticky. I hope it stays cool for a while.

September 1   School starts in four days…yuck. If the weather then is as miserable as it is today, I might not even go. Actually, I love the first day of school because I get to see everyone and it's so busy we don't have much work.

October 1   The fall colors have been spectacular, and today is a perfect day to enjoy them. The sky is blue, there are just a few clouds, and the sun is bright. I feel sorry for people who don't have trees that change color in the fall.

November 1   Winter is definitely here. It's cold, gray, and in general, nasty. The temperature is still in the 20°s, and I'm not looking forward to school at all. I have to walk to school, and I hate getting there wet.

December 1   When December rolls around, everyone in school starts thinking about the holidays. This year, everyone is thinking about the weather. We have had the snowiest winter in history. It's like living in Alaska. Two feet of snow fell last night, and there was already a foot on the ground. Pretty soon, we'll have to dig tunnels to get around.

GO

9 **What can you conclude about where the writer of this journal lives?**

A It is usually warm.

B It is usually cold.

C It has good weather.

D It has four seasons.

10 **What is the "January thaw"?**

F A surprising cold spell that usually takes place in January

G An unusually cold January

H A surprising warm spell that usually takes place in January

J An unusually warm winter

11 **How do the journal entries change from January to December?**

A They focus less on the weather than on the writer's feelings.

B They become much shorter.

C They talk more about the writer's family.

D They focus more on the weather than on the writer's feelings.

12 **To Ashihiro, the weather in July is —**

F cooler than usual.

G too hot and sticky.

H just right for outdoor activities.

J better than in the fall.

13 **How does the writer feel about the first day of school?**

A Bored about school

B Excited to go

C Sad that summer is over

D Happy to go to a new school

14 **What does the writer mean in the March first entry when he says his "computer will get a good workout"?**

F He will work hard to earn money to buy a computer.

G He will go to the gym before using his computer.

H He will spend the day using the computer.

J He will work out instead of using his computer.

15 **How does Ashihiro get to school?**

A By walking

B By school bus

C By public bus

D By car

16 **In the entry for September first, what does the word "miserable" mean?**

F Pleasant

G Unusual

H Usual

J Unpleasant

STOP

Example   **Directions:** Read the passage. Find the best answer to each question that follows the passage.

An unusual presidential election took place in 1789; it was the first election in the history of the United States. General George Washington ran without opposition and was chosen *unanimously* by the electors from every state. Ironically, Washington almost refused to run for office!	**A What is the meaning of the word "unanimously" in this passage?** A By most electors B By a few electors C By all electors D By exactly half the electors

Skim the passage so you have an understanding of what it is about. Then skim the questions. Answer the easiest questions first, and look back at the passage to find the answer.

Practice

Here is a passage about a misunderstanding among family members. Read the passage and then do numbers 1 through 7 on page 29.

A Family's Fright

The Dunn family and friends had gathered for a barbecue. Amy and her friend Nicole were the only young people, and they soon tired of the adult conversation, so they went off to amuse themselves. They practiced twirling a metal rod that regularly fell with a loud clang, causing the people on the porch to jump at each crash.

"You kids, go play on the sand where that thing will not make so much noise," Amy's mother said impatiently.

"On the sand across the street, or on the sand down the way?" Amy asked.

"Wherever," was the absentminded answer, and she turned back to the conversation.

As darkness fell on the pleasant evening, the guests began to leave. Someone asked about the girls. "Oh, they must be in the house," Amy's mother answered with a shrug.

"I don't see them," someone else called back.

That was enough to have Mrs. Dunn on her feet in an instant. "Aim-eee, Ni-cole," she called upstairs and down, in the front yard and back. She grabbed a flashlight and raced out of the house and down the street, thoroughly frightened now.

The others waited and watched for the beam of light to pierce the darkness, signaling that the three were on their way back. It seemed like hours, but was only minutes when they appeared at the end of the street.

Amy's mother put an arm around each girl. "Don't ever do that to me again, please."

"But, Mom, you said we could go down there," Amy protested.

"You knew better than to stay so long…" The sentence remained unfinished, but all three knew what she meant. The girls' protests and explanations also dissolved in the hug. All three were laughing as they approached the house. The adults on the porch were mystified, but their relief was great enough to keep them quiet.

GO

1   What would be another good title for this story?

    A "A Close Call"

    B "Kids Will Be Kids"

    C "A Family Gathering"

    D "A Bad Decision"

2   Why did Amy's mother tell the girls to go play in another place?

    F They were being noisy.

    G She did not want them out too late.

    H The other adults asked her to.

    J There were no other young people there.

3   Why did the girls stop trying to explain why they had gone so far away?

    A They did not care what Mrs. Dunn thought.

    B They did not have a good reason for staying out so late.

    C They knew they were going to be punished anyway.

    D They realized how worried Mrs. Dunn had been and how relieved she was now.

4   Which of these sentences would best fit at the end of the story?

    F The other adults didn't think Mrs. Dunn handled the situation very well.

    G Nicole called her mother and asked to go home right away.

    H Amy and Nicole decided to be more careful the next time they went to play.

    J Mrs. Dunn was too embarrassed to visit with the other people.

5   The girls wandered off because they —

    A wanted to see the beach.

    B were looking for a kitten.

    C were waiting to eat.

    D were bored.

6   When Mrs. Dunn said "Wherever," it showed that she —

    F wasn't really paying attention.

    G wanted the children to go away.

    H was worried about the children.

    J hadn't heard what the girls said.

7   This story began —

    A in the morning.

    B around sunset.

    C around noon.

    D late in the night.

GO

A Stupid Thing to Do

"Is that you, Enrique?" called Mr. Torres from his big chair in front of the television.

"Yeah, it's me, Dad," answered Enrique as he shut the front door behind him.

"Come in here a minute, Son, I want to talk to you," said Mr. Torres.

Enrique sighed and slowly walked toward his father with his hands in his pockets. "I really need to do something in my room, Dad."

"Listen, Enrique. Isn't it a little late for you to be coming home from Lloyd Carlson's house? I know it's a Friday night, and there is no school tomorrow, but I don't like you out on the streets at this hour."

"Hey, Dad, the Carlsons just live in the next block. It's not like I've been walking all over town," replied Enrique, gesturing with his hands.

"What's that on your hands, Son?" asked Mr. Torres.

Enrique looked at his hands and saw streaks of blue paint. "Oh, Lloyd and I were working on some models. I guess I wasn't very careful with the paint."

"Okay, Enrique, off to bed. We'll talk about this more tomorrow. I don't want you out on the streets when it gets this late, even if it's just a block away. Things happen."

Mr. Torres turned off the television and sat in his chair thinking about his son. He sighed, then he went out to the garage to see if the door was closed before he went to bed. He noticed that the can of blue spray paint was not on the shelf where it belonged.

The next morning, Mr. Torres called the Carlsons on the telephone. When he finished speaking to Mrs. Carlson, he hung up the phone and sat drinking a cup of coffee until Enrique came into the kitchen for breakfast.

"Well, good morning, Son," said Mr. Torres with a smile. "You and Lloyd are in for a big surprise next Saturday. There's a very special event taking place in town, and the Carlsons and I have signed you two boys up."

Enrique's face lit up. "What is it, Dad? A Bike-a-thon? A basketball game? Is a celebrity coming to town?"

"No, Son," said Mr. Torres. "None of those things. It's our city's third annual Paint the Town Day. About a thousand people are getting together to paint over graffiti that has been spray painted on walls, fences, and buildings. The only celebrity you're likely to see is the mayor, who is handing out 5,000 gallons of paint and brushes for this project."

Enrique's face fell. "You know, huh?"

"Yes, Enrique. Lloyd's parents thought you boys were over here last night. When I told them I thought you were over there, we figured out what you had done. My first impulse was to call the police, but Mr. Carlson suggested we give you one more chance. On the phone this morning we came up with this idea as a suitable way for you boys to pay the community back for what you have done," said his father. "Graffiti makes our city look bad and costs a lot of money to clean up. So next Saturday, you and Lloyd are going to put in a long day's work."

"Okay, Dad. It was a stupid thing to do, and I'm really sorry. Lloyd and I never did anything like that before, and I promise we won't ever do it again. Next Saturday, we'll be the two best painters in town. You can count on it."

GO

8 Why did Mr. Torres want to talk to Enrique when he came in the door on Friday night?

 F He had a surprise for Enrique.

 G He wanted some company.

 H Enrique was late coming home.

 J Enrique had blue paint on his hands.

9 How did Mr. Torres feel when he saw the can of blue spray paint was gone?

 A Suspicious

 B Relieved

 C Angry

 D Sad

10 "Paint the Town" is an example of —

 F a way to punish young people who have done bad things.

 G a way to celebrate the founding of the town.

 H an opportunity for people to paint their houses with the town's paint.

 J a community project to make the town a better place to live.

11 In this story, what is a "fitting punishment"?

 A One that is easy for the boys to do

 B One that fits the boys' plans

 C One that suits the crime

 D One that is difficult for the boys to do

12 What do Mr. Torres and the Carlsons hope to do with their plan?

 F Teach Enrique and Lloyd to be responsible for what they have done

 G Make the boys angry because they have been caught

 H Help the boys understand the importance of coming home on time

 J Make the boys stay home at night and do their homework

13 Why does Mr. Torres worry about Enrique?

 A His school grades are getting lower.

 B He often gets in trouble with Lloyd.

 C Bad things can happen late at night.

 D The boys need their sleep.

14 When Mr. Torres says he has a surprise for the boys, Enrique —

 F thinks it is something fun to do.

 G worries that he has been caught.

 H wants to call Lloyd to let him know.

 J becomes angry because he has been punished.

15 How does Enrique feel when he learns he is going to "Paint the Town"?

 A Relieved because he hasn't been caught

 B Sorry for doing the wrong thing

 C Angry because he is being punished

 D Annoyed that his father suspected him

The Ocean

Nearly three-fourths of the earth is covered by the oceans. Traditionally, there are said to be five oceans: Atlantic, Pacific, Indian, Arctic, and Antarctic. In reality, all are interconnected, and people, fish, and sea mammals move easily among them. The boundaries of the oceans are loosely determined by islands and land masses, and the terms sea, gulf, and bay are used for subdivisions of the oceans.

Ocean water is salty because of dissolved minerals, and it is the nourishing environment for a host of living things. Plants use the dissolved chemicals that are washed into the oceans for their growth. Tiny animals eat the plants, and larger animals eat them. People eventually eat these large fish, so, in a sense, the minerals in ocean water also nourish us.

Oceans are not alone in being salty. Several "seas"—the Dead Sea, the Caspian Sea, and the Great Salt Lake—are also salty. Dissolved minerals flow into these inland seas, which do not have outlets with other bodies of water. When the sun evaporates the water in these lakes, the concentration of minerals rises, making the lakes salty.

The saltiness in oceans and lakes varies greatly from place to place. Places where the water is confined by islands or peninsulas are saltier than the open water. In the open water, the wind and currents keep the minerals from becoming too concentrated in one place.

Ocean water moves constantly because of currents, wind, and tides. Currents are great rivers within the oceans. One of the best known is the Gulf Stream, which is warm and moves along the southern coast of the United States. Tides are movements of water determined by the positions of the sun, moon, and earth. The gravitational pull of the sun and moon make the water move toward and away from the land in a regular pattern. Wind moves water irregularly, as anyone can tell from watching the waves swell up, turn into a curve, and splash down in a foamy spray.

Humans are closely attached to the ocean. Oceanographers study it and plan ways for people to use it better. Ecologists worry that we will pollute the oceans and damage the fragile life there. Vacationers are soothed by the sights and sounds of the ocean and beach. Sportsmen test themselves against its fish. The ocean is interesting, entertaining, mysterious, and absolutely necessary for life on earth.

GO ▷

16 **What causes movement of water in the oceans?**

F Concentrated minerals left by evaporation

G Natural weather events

H Fish and people sailing in boats

J Rivers at the bottom of all the oceans

17 **Why is the water in the Dead Sea, the Caspian Sea, and the Great Salt Lake saltier than the ocean?**

A They are warmer than the oceans.

B The land around them is saltier.

C They are smaller than the other oceans.

D There is no outlet for their waters.

18 **According to this article, the oceans are necessary for —**

F life.

G travel.

H fun.

J communication.

19 **If you wanted to learn more about the ocean, you should —**

A read a fishing or boating magazine.

B look up the definition of "currents" in the dictionary.

C check the library card catalog under the topic "ocean."

D find the encyclopedia entry titled "water."

20 **Based on what you have read in the passage, an appropriate name for the earth would be —**

F The Desert Planet.

G The Cloud Planet.

H The Evaporation Planet.

J The Water Planet.

21 **Which statement is an *opinion* in the article?**

A There are five oceans: Atlantic, Pacific, Indian, Arctic, and Antarctic.

B The ocean is interesting, entertaining, mysterious, and necessary.

C Saltiness increases as evaporation occurs.

D The water of landlocked seas is saltier than ocean water.

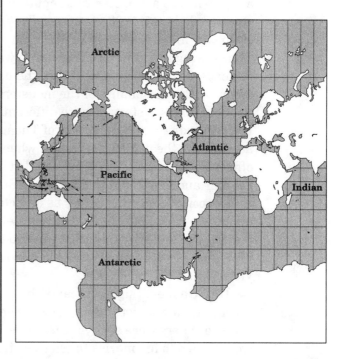

Example   Directions: Read the selection then mark the answer you think is correct.

A group of people stood around a puddle on the ground. From the puddle spilled a small stream of water. They were all amazed, for the puddle and stream had come from nowhere. During the night, a spring had appeared in the park, and no one knew what had caused it.

A   The people were probably —

A frightened.
B curious.
C angry.
D elated.

Here is a passage about two actors who could terrorize an audience. Read the story and then do numbers 1 through 6 on page 35.

Horror movies today are filled with special effects created by computers and mechanical devices. In the early years of film, however, there were no such artificial methods. The actors themselves had to frighten the audience, and the two who were the best at it were Lon Chaney and Bela Lugosi.

The son of deaf parents, Lon Chaney learned Sign Language early in his life and became adept at making himself known through gestures and pantomime. He had little formal education, but at that time—he was born in 1883—an education wasn't as important as it is today. He worked at odd jobs around his home in Colorado Springs, Colorado, and became interested in the theater while working as a stage hand. Chaney tried his hand at playwriting and vaudeville, eventually working his way to Hollywood.

In the *Miracle Man*, which was released in 1919, Lon Chaney made his first appearance as a monster. His reputation grew enormously when he played Quasimodo in the 1923 version of *The Hunchback of Notre Dame*, and he went on to star in other successful films. Chaney only had one speaking role, since films during this era were silent, and was able to capture his audience through the expert application of makeup, the use of gestures, and an uncanny knack for adopting the personality of the monsters he played.

Bela Lugosi's story is quite different. Born in eastern Europe in 1884, Lugosi studied at the Academy of Theatrical Art in Budapest. He worked as an actor in the theatre for years, and when World War I broke out, served as an officer in the Hungarian army. He fled his country in the turmoil that followed the war and emigrated to the United States.

Lugosi resumed his career as an actor in both plays and films after he arrived in New York. He was moderately successful, but he achieved stardom playing the vampire in the 1931 movie *Dracula*. He starred in a string of horror films that remain cult classics even to this day among late-night television viewers and old movie fans.

Like Chaney, Lugosi "became" his characters. With his eastern European accent and mysterious looks, he was the perfect Dracula. In his other films, his evil characters were always more believable than anyone else's, and crowds were drawn to his movies to see this star who appeared to be the heart of evil.

GO

1 Which of these did Lon Chaney and Bela Lugosi have in common?

   A They both studied at a famous school of theater.

   B Their parents helped them to become actors.

   C They both had unusual accents.

   D They were born within a year of each other.

2 According to the passage, Lon Chaney —

   F got his start acting in New York City.

   G made most of his films during the silent era.

   H starred with Bela Lugosi in just one movie.

   J first appeared in the film *The Hunchback of Notre Dame.*

3 Which of these probably helped Bela Lugosi get the part of Dracula?

   A Lugosi had experience in the war.

   B Both the character Dracula and Lugosi were the same height.

   C The Dracula character was from eastern Europe, so Lugosi sounded like him.

   D Lugosi was popular among television viewers.

4 The writer of this passage believes that —

   F horror movies today depend more on special effects than acting ability.

   G silent movies are better than movies where the actors can speak.

   H theatrical training is an important ingredient in stage success.

   J horror movies are the best kind of film.

5 This passage says that Lon Chaney had "an uncanny knack for adopting the personality of the monsters he played." The word *uncanny* means —

   A beyond the ordinary.

   B eastern European.

   C natural.

   D limited.

6 The author suggests that Bela Lugosi was so successful because —

   F his accent sounded evil.

   G fans were less sophisticated years ago.

   H he appeared to be the heart of evil.

   J films are too technical today.

GO

Butch's Discount City
1410 Main Street

Annual Summer Clearance
As the temperatures rise, the prices fall!

Deluxe Ceiling Fan
with light kit
• 3-speed
• quiet
• reversible
only $35.97

Garden Rain Sprinkler
Model 3600
"Makes your lawn
beautiful"
was $8.96
reduced to $4.97

Boys' Short-Sleeved
T-Shirts
• solid colors
• s-m-l-xl
Regularly $3.00
Reduced to $1.50

Select group of ladies'
summer shoes and sandals
(on racks)
Name brands
40% off regular prices

Bertha's Bargain Bonanza
5331 Seventh Avenue

Always the best buys in town! (Sale prices good through Saturday)

All boys' shorts and shirts
on sale now, sizes 4-18
Giant blowout
25% off regular prices

Fourth of July
paper goods
Everything must go
half price

All electric fans in stock
now reduced 10%
(regularly $9.99-$49.99)

Flower seeds
Plant a late summer garden
(this year's seeds) 79¢ each

Store Hours: 9 A.M. - 7 P.M., Monday through Saturday

GO

7 What time of year is it when these ads might appear in the newspaper?

A early spring

B middle to late summer

C winter

D just before Thanksgiving

8 What does "reversible" mean in the deluxe ceiling fan ad at Butch's?

F The light and the fan can run independently of each other.

G The fan can be turned off and on.

H The blades of the fan can be made to turn in opposite directions.

J The fan will create heat in the winter.

9 Both stores' advertisements stress —

A good service.

B excellent location.

C lengthy store hours.

D bargain prices.

10 You would most likely find these advertisements in a —

F gardening book.

G national magazine.

H telephone book.

J local newspaper.

11 In the ad for Butch's Discount City, the line "As the temperatures rise, the prices fall!" means that—

A Butch's usually has a sale in the summer.

B prices are reduced any time the temperature reaches 100 degrees.

C Butch's has lower prices than Bertha's.

D Butch's does not have sales in cool weather.

12 Which of these is an *opinion* in Bertha's ad?

F Plant a late summer garden

G Sale prices good through Saturday

H Always the best buys in town

J Half price

13 Which of these does *not* have an exact price specified?

A Deluxe ceiling fan

B Ladies summer shoes and sandals

C Boys short-sleeved t-shirts

D Garden Rain Sprinkler

14 The sale at Butch's Discount City is —

F a yearly event.

G a weekly event.

H a monthly event.

J a daily event.

GO

Can fish smell fishermen?

Some people go fishing to enjoy the peace, quiet, and beauty of nature. Some love to catch fish for a tasty meal. Others, however, fish for sport and will go to great lengths to catch the most or the largest fish. Huge amounts of money and fabulous prizes are offered at some fishing contests. The bait, the equipment, the location all are important factors, but there is one additional thing to consider: fish have a remarkable sense of smell.

Bass have a well-developed *olfactory* sense. The older they get, the more they use their sense of smell. Catfish, trout, and other fish can also smell very well. Some things smell good to fish, and some things smell bad. Fishermen, then, must learn to avoid smells that turn away fish if they are going to win a competition.

Chewing tobacco and smoking, in addition to being bad for you, create an odor that fish don't like. Gasoline spilled in or on a boat will also repel fish. One of the worst turn-offs for fish is the chemical L-serine, which is present in human perspiration. This means fisherman should bathe before they go fishing and wear clean clothes.

Scientists have found that all people produce L-serine, but some create more than others. A group of the top professional tournament fishermen have been tested, and they seem to have very little L-serine in their perspiration.

There is no evidence that fish like the same perfumes that humans find attractive, however. Most tournament fishermen use plain soap, without perfume, to wash. They even take soap with them on their boats. Sporting goods stores also sell a spray that masks human odors and adds a smell that is supposed to appeal to fish.

Not everyone is a tournament fisherman, but most people like to catch fish when they go out on the lake. If you expect to catch fish, you can wear your old clothes and favorite hat, but be sure you are clean. Avoid tobacco—which everyone should do anyway—and wash off spilled gasoline. Don't chase away fish with bad smells.

GO

15 Which words from the article tell that some people don't care whether they catch fish or not?

A ...enjoy the peace, quiet, and beauty...

B ...huge amounts of money...

C ...catch fish for a tasty meal.

D ...most people like to catch fish...

16 As bass get older, they —

F learn to like the smells of human beings.

G become more like trout and catfish.

H have less L-serine in their system.

J depend more on their sense of smell.

17 What would be the best thing to do to answer Number 16?

A Look closely at the first paragraph and then the last paragraph.

B Read the title and think about what it means.

C Skim the passage and look for the key words "bass" and "older."

D Look up L-serine in the dictionary or encyclopedia.

18 What natural human odor do fish not like?

F Gasoline

G L-serine

H Chemical attractants

J Perfume

19 This passage is an example of which type of writing?

A Providing information

B Expressing an opinion

C Fiction

D A review

20 The author probably included the first sentence of the third paragraph because —

F winning a fishing tournament is difficult if you smoke.

G L-serine and tobacco have many of the same ingredients.

H gasoline spilled in a boat will chase fish away.

J in addition to scaring off fish, tobacco can harm your health.

21 In this passage, the word *olfactory* has something to do with —

A fishing.

B bass.

C age.

D smelling.

22 This passage is mostly about —

F fishing tournaments.

G an important fishing tip.

H why people enjoy fishing.

J differences between people and fish.

GO

That Trophy Season

From their team name, the Aardvarks, to their uniforms, shorts and bowling shirts, the Lincoln School baseball team was unusual. They had gone years without winning a game, and because their school was so small, it had both girls and boys playing on the same team. Most of all, however, was the team attitude: they loved baseball. Every team they played admitted that, no matter how bad they were, the Aardvarks played their hearts out and were good sports.

A few years ago, however, something changed. A set of twins, Dot and Dash Morse, had started school in the fall, and to say they were great ball players was an understatement. They were fabulous. Dash could pitch like a high school player, and Dot played shortstop like she had been born there. Moreover, they had a great sense of humor, obviously inherited from their parents, who had named their children after the Morse code signals. They poked fun at everyone and everything, but nothing pleased them more than making fun of themselves.

All of this came as a surprise to Coach McNally, who had heard nothing about the Morse twins until the first day of spring training. He knew they were good students, as was everyone else on the Aardvarks baseball team, and welcomed them to tryouts. Within a few minutes, however, they had him scratching his head. He couldn't believe his good fortune: these two kids were the best he had ever seen. What was even better was that they had a great attitude toward the game and seemed to be infecting the other players. For the first time in years, Coach McNally actually began to think about winning games.

Throughout spring training, Coach McNally downplayed his squad's ability. All the players knew this was going to be a special year, but when asked about his team, the coach just said they were going to enjoy the game as much as ever. In his heart, however, he couldn't wait for the season to start.

On opening day, the Aardvarks faced the Mountaineers, a traditional powerhouse. Everyone in the stands anticipated the annual blowout, but when Dash threw his first pitch, the sound of his strike whacking the catcher's mitt got everyone's attention. And when the first three Mountaineers went down in order, even the opposing players suspected this was not going to be business as usual.

Dot was up first for the Aardvarks, and just like in the movies, sent a ball into the stands. The Aardvark fans went absolutely wild. It was the first time in anyone's memory they had a real reason to cheer. By the time the game was over, everyone at the game knew that the Aardvarks were the team to beat. Not only had Dot and Dash dazzled the crowd, but the other Aardvarks had played like they had never done before.

The rest of the season was a continuation of that first game. The Aardvarks won every game, and none of them were even close. Dot and Dash broke every school baseball record, and in the championship tournament, the Aardvarks swept the trophy. To Coach McNally, the whole season, and especially the tournament, was like a dream.

That summer, the Morse family moved away, and not much more was heard of Dot and Dash. Every once in a while, someone would see their names in the newspaper, including a clipping from Japan, where they had led a team from a U.S. Army base to the national championship.

As for the rest of the Aardvarks, something had changed forever. Although they never again had a perfect season, they were always in contention. The Aardvarks still loved the game as much as ever, their grades never slipped, and they still needed girls and boys to field a squad. That championship season had made a difference in the Aardvarks, however, and whenever they walked onto a baseball field, they felt they had a good chance to win the game.

GO

23 **The author says that the twins poke fun at themselves to show that —**

    A Coach McNally believes his team can win the championship this year.

    B even though the twins are good, other players contribute to the team.

    C a sense of humor is important to playing baseball.

    D they don't think they are better than other people.

24 **Based on what you read in the passage, which pair of words fits in this sentence?**

The Morse twins _____ the Aardvarks and _____ the team's confidence.

    F influenced...improved

    G joined...absorbed

    H left...diminished

    J abandoned...devastated

25 **Which of these explains why Coach McNally downplayed his squad's ability?**

    A He knew the Morse twins would leave the team after this season.

    B He had no confidence the team would do well during the season.

    C He wanted to surprise the other teams with the Aardvark's improved abilities.

    D He liked the team better when they always lost their games.

26 **Which of these best describes what happens in the passage?**

    F A school's baseball team has a history of enjoying the game but not playing well.

    G Two outstanding players improve a baseball team that is usually a loser.

    H A school baseball coach gets the championship team he always dreamed about.

    J The team that is usually a powerhouse loses a season opener to a far worse team.

GO >

For numbers 27 through 30, choose the best answer to the question.

27 Which of these sentences states a fact?

  A Most people change jobs several times during their lives.

  B The best job you will ever have is your first job.

  C The most important thing a job provides is the friendship of your co-workers.

  D Rich people do easier work than poor people.

28 Benjamin is writing a story about his family's history. Which of these is most likely to be found in the middle of the story?

  F Today, the family is spread all over the the United States, but most of us live in the Northeast.

  G Although Spain had long been their home, several members of the family decided to come to the United States around the time of the Civil War.

  H Our family name can be easily traced back for hundreds of years because the majority of the family lived in the same region of Spain.

  J Because of a scrapbook my grandmother has been keeping, future generations will be able to look upon our past.

29 Which of these is most likely taken from a legend?

  A The caves were formed by water actually dissolving the rocks over many thousands of years.

  B No one has ever found the treasure, but the locals insist it is somewhere deep inside the cave.

  C The first settlers in the area, Native Americans, discovered the caves.

  D I can remember the first time my family visited the caves.

30 His guilt was a heavy burden he would bear throughout his life.

What does this statement really mean?

  F He was guilty of stealing something valuable.

  G Feeling guilty made him eat a lot.

  H His strength allowed him to carry out crimes.

  J Being guilty was something he thought about often and it bothered him.

To the Student:

These tests will give you a chance to put the tips you have learned to work.

A few last reminders…

- Be sure you understand all the directions before you begin each test. You may ask the teacher questions about the directions if you do not understand them.
- Work as quickly as you can during each test.
- When you change an answer, be sure to erase your first mark completely.

- You can guess at an answer or skip difficult items and go back to them later.
- Use the tips you have learned whenever you can.
- It is OK to be a little nervous. You may even do better.

Now that you have completed the lessons in this unit, you are on your way to scoring high!

STUDENT'S NAME		SCHOOL
LAST	FIRST	MI	TEACHER

FEMALE ◯   MALE ◯

BIRTH DATE

MONTH	DAY	YEAR
JAN	0 0	0
FEB	1 1	1
MAR	2 2	2
APR	3 3	3
MAY	4	4
JUN	5	5 5
JUL	6	6 6
AUG	7	7 7
SEP	8	8 8
OCT	9	9 9
NOV		
DEC		

GRADE

⑤   ⑥   ⑦

(Name grid bubbles: A B C D E F G H I J K L M N O P Q R S T U V W X Y Z)

PART 1   VOCABULARY

E1 Ⓐ Ⓑ Ⓒ Ⓓ	6 Ⓕ Ⓖ Ⓗ Ⓙ	13 Ⓐ Ⓑ Ⓒ Ⓓ	20 Ⓕ Ⓖ Ⓗ Ⓙ	26 Ⓕ Ⓖ Ⓗ Ⓙ	31 Ⓐ Ⓑ Ⓒ Ⓓ
E2 Ⓕ Ⓖ Ⓗ Ⓙ	7 Ⓐ Ⓑ Ⓒ Ⓓ	14 Ⓕ Ⓖ Ⓗ Ⓙ	21 Ⓐ Ⓑ Ⓒ Ⓓ	27 Ⓐ Ⓑ Ⓒ Ⓓ	32 Ⓕ Ⓖ Ⓗ Ⓙ
1 Ⓐ Ⓑ Ⓒ Ⓓ	8 Ⓕ Ⓖ Ⓗ Ⓙ	15 Ⓐ Ⓑ Ⓒ Ⓓ	22 Ⓕ Ⓖ Ⓗ Ⓙ	28 Ⓕ Ⓖ Ⓗ Ⓙ	33 Ⓐ Ⓑ Ⓒ Ⓓ
2 Ⓕ Ⓖ Ⓗ Ⓙ	9 Ⓐ Ⓑ Ⓒ Ⓓ	16 Ⓕ Ⓖ Ⓗ Ⓙ	23 Ⓐ Ⓑ Ⓒ Ⓓ	29 Ⓐ Ⓑ Ⓒ Ⓓ	34 Ⓕ Ⓖ Ⓗ Ⓙ
3 Ⓐ Ⓑ Ⓒ Ⓓ	10 Ⓕ Ⓖ Ⓗ Ⓙ	17 Ⓐ Ⓑ Ⓒ Ⓓ	24 Ⓕ Ⓖ Ⓗ Ⓙ	30 Ⓕ Ⓖ Ⓗ Ⓙ	35 Ⓐ Ⓑ Ⓒ Ⓓ
4 Ⓕ Ⓖ Ⓗ Ⓙ	11 Ⓐ Ⓑ Ⓒ Ⓓ	18 Ⓕ Ⓖ Ⓗ Ⓙ	25 Ⓐ Ⓑ Ⓒ Ⓓ		
5 Ⓐ Ⓑ Ⓒ Ⓓ	12 Ⓕ Ⓖ Ⓗ Ⓙ	19 Ⓐ Ⓑ Ⓒ Ⓓ			

PART 2   READING COMPREHENSION

E1 Ⓐ Ⓑ Ⓒ Ⓓ	6 Ⓕ Ⓖ Ⓗ Ⓙ	12 Ⓕ Ⓖ Ⓗ Ⓙ	18 Ⓕ Ⓖ Ⓗ Ⓙ	24 Ⓕ Ⓖ Ⓗ Ⓙ	30 Ⓕ Ⓖ Ⓗ Ⓙ
1 Ⓐ Ⓑ Ⓒ Ⓓ	7 Ⓐ Ⓑ Ⓒ Ⓓ	13 Ⓐ Ⓑ Ⓒ Ⓓ	19 Ⓐ Ⓑ Ⓒ Ⓓ	25 Ⓐ Ⓑ Ⓒ Ⓓ	31 Ⓐ Ⓑ Ⓒ Ⓓ
2 Ⓕ Ⓖ Ⓗ Ⓙ	8 Ⓕ Ⓖ Ⓗ Ⓙ	14 Ⓕ Ⓖ Ⓗ Ⓙ	20 Ⓕ Ⓖ Ⓗ Ⓙ	26 Ⓕ Ⓖ Ⓗ Ⓙ	32 Ⓕ Ⓖ Ⓗ Ⓙ
3 Ⓐ Ⓑ Ⓒ Ⓓ	9 Ⓐ Ⓑ Ⓒ Ⓓ	15 Ⓐ Ⓑ Ⓒ Ⓓ	21 Ⓐ Ⓑ Ⓒ Ⓓ	27 Ⓐ Ⓑ Ⓒ Ⓓ	33 Ⓐ Ⓑ Ⓒ Ⓓ
4 Ⓕ Ⓖ Ⓗ Ⓙ	10 Ⓕ Ⓖ Ⓗ Ⓙ	16 Ⓕ Ⓖ Ⓗ Ⓙ	22 Ⓕ Ⓖ Ⓗ Ⓙ	28 Ⓕ Ⓖ Ⓗ Ⓙ	34 Ⓕ Ⓖ Ⓗ Ⓙ
5 Ⓐ Ⓑ Ⓒ Ⓓ	11 Ⓐ Ⓑ Ⓒ Ⓓ	17 Ⓐ Ⓑ Ⓒ Ⓓ	23 Ⓐ Ⓑ Ⓒ Ⓓ	29 Ⓐ Ⓑ Ⓒ Ⓓ	35 Ⓐ Ⓑ Ⓒ Ⓓ

Part 1   Vocabulary

Examples **Directions:** For item E1, find the word that means the same or almost the same as the underlined word. For item E2, mark the answer you think is correct. Then, follow the directions for each part of this test.

E1 daring rescue A foolish B rapid C brave D painstaking	**E2 Which of these probably comes from the Old English word *fikol* meaning *deceitful*?** F frank G infinity H definitely J fickle

For numbers 1-13, find the word or words that mean the same or almost the same as the underlined word.

1   slight gesture

A distance
B movement
C build
D angle

5   To support is to —

A not enjoy
B not play
C let down
D hold up

2   tightly bound

F boxed
G released
H matched
J tied

6   Cardiac refers to the —

F brain
G stomach
H heart
J foot

3   deny him permission

A allow
B give
C offer
D refuse

7   A cottage is a —

A castle
B garage
C huge barn
D small house

4   link the ideas

F separate
G join
H identify
J like

8   To irritate is to —

F contact
G bother
H chase
J embarrass

GO

9   Georgina <u>stumbled</u> on the path.

Stumbled means —

A   jumped
B   walked
C   ran
D   tripped

10   Your <u>response</u> was too short.

Response means the same as —

F   answer
G   story
H   paragraph
J   problem

11   The hotel had a wonderful <u>staff</u>.

A staff is a —

A   swimming pool
B   group of workers
C   lobby
D   restaurant

12   Donna told us a <u>brief</u> story.

Brief means —

F   sad
G   funny
H   long
J   short

13   Ken <u>stored</u> the children's toys.

Stored means —

A   found
B   wrapped
C   put away
D   bought

For numbers 14-19, find the word that means the opposite of the underlined word.

14   the <u>proper</u> tools

F   incorrect
G   useful
H   appropriate
J   adjustable

15   might <u>detain</u>

A   hold
B   release
C   enlighten
D   restrain

16   seems <u>colorful</u>

F   pale
G   vibrant
H   delightful
J   humid

17   <u>reveal</u> the truth

A   make known
B   look for
C   disbelieve
D   carefully hide

18   <u>persist</u> for a while

F   continue
G   resist
H   cease
J   follow

19   <u>sufficient</u> for now

A   too expensive
B   too little
C   enough
D   unnecessary

GO

For numbers 20-23, choose the word that correctly completes <u>both</u> sentences.

20 The _____ was a few minutes late.

Gina will _____ hard for the race.

F bus
G practice
H train
J plane

21 How much _____ do you have?

Remember to _____ your wet shoes.

A money
B change
C adjust
D wind

22 The worker carried a _____ .

Let's _____ some apples.

F pick
G bake
H shovel
J ladder

23 Cheryl put the _____ on the shelf.

The swimming _____ was just broken.

A video
B pool
C package
D record

24 | What <u>grade</u> did you get in math?

In which sentence does the word **grade** mean the same thing as in the sentence above?

F This store offers only the top grade of fruits and vegetables.
G The best way to improve my grade is to study harder.
H The grade on this hill is so steep that trucks find it difficult.
J Mrs. Irwin will grade our papers today.

25 | Randi made her <u>point</u> by giving several examples.

In which sentence does the word **point** mean the same thing as in the sentence above?

A Grant broke the point on his pencil.
B The point of his argument is that the park is good for the town.
C The point of the compass changed as the boat made a turn.
D Can you point to the right store?

For numbers 26 and 27, choose the answer that best defines the underlined part.

26 <u>pre</u>judge   <u>pre</u>school

F after
G less than
H more than
J before

27 cloud<u>y</u>   itch<u>y</u>

A inclined to be
B not
C much
D about to become

47

GO

28 Which of these words probably comes from the Latin word *fimbri* meaning *a border*?

   F family
   G fringe
   H image
   J feminine

29 Which of these words probably comes from the Old French word *renc* meaning *row*?

   A wrench
   B rich
   C rank
   D prank

30 We made sure the house was _____ before we left for vacation.

Which of these words means the house was locked up tightly?

   F sincere
   G vacated
   H secure
   J inevitable

31 It began to _____ so we packed everything up and went home.

Which of these words means it began to rain just a little?

   A drizzle
   B downpour
   C dazzle
   D thwart

Read the paragraph. Find the word below the paragraph that fits best in each numbered blank.

     Inventions don't have to be __(32)__ to be successful. A good example of a simple invention is the water-filled barrels that serve as protective __(33)__ at a highway bridge or overpass. Another is the Frisbee®, a toy that sells millions of __(34)__ a year. And of course, there's the ultimate in simplicity, the clothespin. These examples demonstrate that clever individuals don't need huge corporations or a research __(35)__ to come up with good ideas.

32 **F** elaborate
     G cancelled
     H comprehensible
     J sincere

33 **A** frontiers
     B barriers
     C parcels
     D testimonials

34 **F** arbors
     G notions
     H licenses
     J units

35 **A** attitude
     B perspective
     C facility
     D harness

STOP

Example   Directions: Read the selection then mark the answer you think is correct.

E1

Alexandra looked at the mess in the kitchen. Someone had gotten into the trash and there was stuff all over the floor. It looked as if a tornado had hit the kitchen. It didn't take her long to figure out who the culprit was. Her dog, Barfley, was huddled up under the dining room table. His chin was on the floor and he had a guilty expression on his face.

A What do you think will happen next?

A Barfley will sniff the trash.

B Alexandra will walk the dog.

C Barfley will run away.

D Alexandra will scold Barfley.

Here is a passage about the part of the universe in which we live. Read the passage and then do numbers 1 through 8 on page 50.

The earth and the other planets in our solar system belong to a spiral galaxy called the Milky Way. The Milky Way is shaped like a disk with "arms" reaching out from a well defined center. Our solar system is far from the center of the galaxy, near the end of one of the arms. In galactic terms, we are way out in the boondocks.

Our solar system is not, however, at the edge of the galaxy. The corona or outermost formation in the Milky Way is at least 200,000 light-years from the center. Since a light-year, the distance traveled by light in one year, is about 5.9 trillion miles, the distance from one side of our galaxy to the other is almost unimaginable!

The stars in the galaxy, and there are many millions of them, are divided into two classifications, Population I and Population II. Population I stars, which are found in the arms of the spiral, contain elements heavier than helium and range in age from a few hundred thousand years to over ten billion years. Our sun is a Population I star.

Population II stars are all approximately 12 to 15 billion years old. They are located near the center of the galaxy and are composed of relatively light elements.

Until about fifty years ago, scientists thought our galaxy was the entire universe. Today, we know that our galaxy is just a small part of it, and that there are millions of other galaxies in the universe.

Trying to map our galaxy is not an easy task. In addition to dealing with millions of stars and huge distances, astronomers must try to "see" through galactic dust. The problem they face is much like the problem you would face looking out a very dirty window and trying to figure out who was walking up the road a mile away.

Scientists solved the problem by measuring the radio waves emitted by the stars. Radio waves pass through the dust and can be measured more accurately than light. Radio astronomy, as this technique is known, allowed scientists to paint a much more precise picture of our galaxy. They found that in addition to solar systems and dust clouds, our galaxy includes a black hole. This structure appears to be a collapsed star that is so dense that it actually absorbs light and attracts anything that comes near it. If an asteroid or a space ship got too close to a black hole, it would disappear into a *void* about which scientists know nothing.

GO

1   According to this passage —

   A   Population II stars are generally older than Population I stars.

   B   Population I stars are generally older than Population II stars.

   C   Population I stars are generally larger than Population II stars.

   D   Population II stars are generally larger than Population I stars.

2   The author probably wrote this passage —

   F   to describe our solar system.

   G   to explain what a light-year is.

   H   to describe what a black hole is.

   J   to explain the structure of the galaxy.

3   What does the phrase "out in the boondocks" mean in this passage?

   A   Near the center of things

   B   Far from the center of things

   C   Poor

   D   Small

4   From this passage, you can conclude that —

   F   the galaxy and the universe are the same.

   G   the number of stars can be counted exactly using radio waves.

   H   distances in space are unimaginable.

   J   spatial measurements are precise.

5   A "void" in this passage is —

   A   a very heavy star.

   B   an unknown region.

   C   a spiral galaxy.

   D   an asteroid.

6   The author compares galactic dust to —

   F   fine particles.

   G   unimaginable distances.

   H   a dirty window.

   J   radio waves.

7   Because of the great distances involved in studying space, scientists —

   A   have a hard time seeing stars through telescopes.

   B   can't use radio waves to study the stars through galactic dust.

   C   know exactly what a black hole is and what causes them.

   D   have a hard time actually proving their ideas are right or wrong.

8   The earth is —

   F   part of the solar system and the galaxy.

   G   part of the solar system but not the galaxy.

   H   part of the galaxy but not the solar system.

   J   part of neither the galaxy nor the solar system.

In this story, a girl and her grandmother make an interesting discovery in the attic on a rainy day. Read the story, then do numbers 9 through 17.

Letters from the Past

It was a cold, rainy afternoon. Mary Lou and her grandmother were in the attic of her grandmother's Iowa farmhouse, entertaining themselves by looking through the contents of a battered, old trunk.

"These old clothes are a riot, Grandma. Did people really wear things like this?" asked Mary Lou smiling.

"They certainly did," replied Grandma. "Your aunts and uncles wore them and thought themselves elegant, indeed."

Mary Lou laughed and pulled an old candy box out of the trunk. She lifted the lid and found a packet of letters tied with string. "These letters look really old, Grandma. See how the envelopes are tattered and yellowed?"

"Look at the stamps, Mary Lou. You couldn't mail a letter today with a one cent stamp on it."

"Who wrote them?" asked Mary Lou, trying to read the flowing, graceful handwriting.

"Well, they are addressed to my mother and father, and the postmark shows they were mailed from Neversink, New York," Grandma noted as she flipped through the envelopes in the packet. "They are all from my father's mother whose name was Anna Thomas. I had forgotten all about them." Grandma removed the string from around the letters. She carefully opened an envelope and removed the letter.

"The writing is very fancy," commented Mary Lou as she stared at the letter.

"Telephones weren't available in Iowa until after 1900. If Anna Thomas wanted to stay in touch with her son and his wife who had moved from New York to Iowa, she had to do so by writing letters. Penmanship was very important, and people took pride in showing a fine hand," said Grandma.

"What does the letter say?" asked Mary Lou. Grandma adjusted her eyeglasses and read:

Dear Children,
I think you must have had a hard time building your house. When I read the newspapers and they told about the snowstorms, I could not sleep nights to think how hard you must have it. Jeanie, I was glad you sent me a lock of your hair. I will send you a lock of mine and wish you would send a lock of Arthur's. I will send you some of my lettuce seed. It is the headed kind. We all call it very good. Take it and cut it fine, put sugar and cream on it. You must have the plants about a foot apart and hoe it like you would cabbage. Write soon and have faith. There is trouble everywhere, and you will overcome yours.
Your loving mother, Anna

When Grandma finished reading, Mary Lou was quiet for a moment and then whispered, "I think she must have missed them a lot and worried about them because they were so far away from her."

"Yes, I'm sure she did. Anna never saw her children again, you know. The trip to Iowa was too much for her, and the children couldn't afford to leave the farm. But she wrote them almost every week, and they wrote back to her. Even though they were more than a thousand miles apart, they remained very close." Grandma looked at Mary Lou and put her arm around her. "We are fortunate to have these letters, Mary Lou. Someday when you have children, I hope you will read the letters to them. Nothing would please me more than to know my grandchildren had the opportunity to learn all about my grandmother's life."

GO

9   What made Mary Lou think the letters were old?

   A They were in the trunk.

   B The stamps were strange.

   C They had pictures with them.

   D They looked old and yellowed.

10   The postmark on an envelope shows —

   F where the letter was mailed.

   G who wrote the letter.

   H where the letter is going.

   J who will receive the letter.

11   Why were grandmother and Mary Lou going through the trunk?

   A They like the attic.

   B The electricity was out.

   C There was not much else to do.

   D It was too hot outside.

12   In this story, "showing a fine hand" means —

   F having good penmanship.

   G having nice hands.

   H dressing with nice gloves.

   J writing often to friends.

13   What surprised Mary Lou?

   A Where the letters came from

   B The way people dressed long ago

   C That her grandmother wanted to go to the attic with her

   D That people wrote to each other rather than using the telephone

14   Who wrote the letters Mary Lou found in the old trunk?

   F Mary Lou's mother

   G The mother and father of Grandma

   H The mother of Grandma's father

   J Mary Lou's grandmother

15   What does the word "elegant" mean in the third paragraph?

   A Very unusual

   B Funny

   C Without many colors

   D Showing good taste

16   In the letter Anna Thomas wrote to her family in Iowa, she said she could not sleep nights because —

   F she had read about the snowstorm in the newspaper.

   G she wanted a lock of her son's hair.

   H she wanted Jeanie to grow lettuce from the seeds she sent.

   J there was trouble everywhere.

17   At the end of the story, Grandma expresses her belief that —

   A Mary Lou should write letters to her very often.

   B she missed her children who lived far away.

   C children should learn about their family's history.

   D letters are the best way to learn about family members.

GO

Can something that tastes so delicious be good for you?

America has given the world many foods, one of which is the pecan. This tasty nut is a wonderful snack plain or roasted, and it adds flavor and crunch to all sorts of dishes. Moreover, pecans are healthful as well as delicious. They are a good source of protein and contain iron, calcium, potassium, phosphorous, magnesium, and B vitamins. They are also high in fiber and unsaturated fat. Unfortunately, pecans are also high in calories—190 calories per ounce—and that makes them fattening if eaten in great quantity.

People in the South have enjoyed finding and eating native pecans for centuries. The earliest French and Spanish explorers found that pecans were a staple part of the Native American diet. In fact, the name pecan comes from an Algonquin word that means "good to eat but with a hard shell." The trees naturally grow along riverbanks in the South. The rushing water carries nuts and deposits them in other places where they can sprout and grow. The warm climate in the South is perfect for pecan trees.

Native pecans are tasty and abundant, but the shells are very hard. Horticulturists have developed more than a thousand different varieties of pecans with thinner shells, called paper shell pecans. All of these varieties are *grafts*, which means a branch from a paper shell tree is attached to a cut made in the trunk of a young native tree. If it grows (or grafts), the other limbs of the native tree are cut off and only the paper shell limb develops. The root system is native, but the limbs and fruit are paper shell. This grafting process is necessary because only nuts from native trees, not paper shell pecan trees, can be planted to produce a new tree.

Most pecans are grown on farms today. The pecan tree farmer has to learn patience because a pecan tree must be six years old before it will bear fruit. A productive pecan farm can produce a thousand pounds of pecans per acre of trees. Georgia produces more of the country's commercial pecan crop than any other state, 46 percent. Texas is second with 26 percent.

Although pecans can be bought in stores year-round, many people plant paper shell pecan trees so they can grow their own nuts. The trees are attractive around a house, provide shade, and produce tasty nuts. In the American South, gathering native pecans is still a favorite fall activity. Families head out to the woods on a sunny afternoon with a picnic basket and a burlap sack. They enjoy their lunch and come home with a sack filled with delicious pecans.

18 **Why must pecan farmers be patient?**

   F If you plant a pecan tree in spring, you won't get nuts until autumn.

   G It takes a long time before a pecan tree grows nuts.

   H It takes a long time to open a pecan shell because it is hard.

   J Picking up pecans from the ground takes a long time.

19 **In this passage, the term "graft" refers to —**

   A taking money illegally.

   B something you do that requires a lot of talent.

   C planting pecan trees.

   D growing a limb from one tree on another tree.

20 **What would grow if you planted a pecan from a paper shell tree?**

   F It would not grow.

   G It would grow a native tree.

   H It would grow roots from a native tree.

   J It would take years to produce nuts.

21 **In this passage, what tone does the author use?**

   A Uncertain

   B Calming

   C Factual

   D Excited

22 **In this passage, a "native tree" is one that —**

   F was planted by Native Americans.

   G was grafted.

   H has thin-shelled nuts.

   J grows naturally.

23 **This passage suggests that —**

   A pecan farmers make more money than other farmers.

   B the pecan is the most healthful nut.

   C pecan shells are tasty.

   D pecans should be eaten in small quantities.

24 **Pecan trees seem to grow best —**

   F where the weather is cold.

   G where the weather is warm.

   H in hot, dry ground.

   J where the wind seems to blow often.

GO

Dragon's Tears

The folklore of China is filled with stories of dragons. In the ancient Chinese stories, dragons are not bad, and young men do not set out on quests to destroy them. Dragon emperors have beautiful daughters who want to find good, kind peasant husbands and live happily ever after on earth. One dragon story takes place in the province of Sichuan, which has twenty-four small lakes called Dragon's Tears. The story of their name is a favorite Chinese legend.

Wen Peng was a good, peasant boy who lived with his widowed mother. He fished and sold his catch to support himself and his mother. One day, he felt an enormous tug on his line. He fought and struggled and finally landed a huge, golden fish. The fish gasped, "Please, let me go, and I will reward you." Wen Peng felt sorry for the creature and returned it to the water. In return, the fish gave him a magic pearl.

With the magic pearl, Wen Peng and his mother had all they needed and were very happy. A jealous neighbor saw their prosperity and became very suspicious. "You are sending your son out to steal," he told Wen Peng's mother. "There is no other way for you to be doing so well." The mother was so frightened that she told the neighbor about the pearl.

This only increased the neighbor's jealousy, and he was determined to get the magic pearl. As soon as Wen Peng came into the house, he and his men grabbed the boy and began to shake him, demanding the pearl. Wen Peng had hidden the pearl in his mouth, and the shaking made him swallow it.

Wen Peng fainted, and when he woke, he asked his mother for water. He drank and drank but could not satisfy his thirst. He finally went down to the river where he had caught the fish. It seemed as if he would drink the river dry.

As darkness came, a huge storm arose. Wen Peng's mother watched in horror as her son slowly turned into a great dragon and started to fly away. She begged him not to go, but a gust of wind carried him into the sky as he called, "I am sorry, Mother. I cannot stay."

"Come back. Come back, my son," she continued to call. The dragon turned sadly, and great tears fell from his fiery eyes. After these drops fell to the ground, they formed the two dozen lakes of Sichuan.

25   Wen Peng can best be described as —

A   reasonable.

B   responsible.

C   greedy.

D   jealous.

26   Wen Peng let the golden fish go because —

F   the fish gave him a pearl.

G   he felt sorry for the fish.

H   he could not eat it.

J   the neighbor came by.

27   Another good title for this story is —

A   "The Boy and the Magic Pearl."

B   "A Good Son."

C   "Don't Go, My Son."

D   "The Boy Who Became A Dragon."

28   This story is a legend about —

F   a boy learning a lesson.

G   why sons should love their mothers.

H   the problems caused by greed.

J   how twenty-four lakes were formed.

29   There is enough information in this story to show that —

A   it could not really happen.

B   people in China think dragons are real.

C   Wen Peng was a bad son.

D   thunder is caused by dragons.

30   The jealous neighbor was determined to have —

F   all the family's money.

G   the magic pearl.

H   the power to turn into a dragon.

J   the golden fish.

31   In order to answer number 30, the best thing to do is —

A   skim the whole story several times.

B   look at the beginning of each paragraph.

C   look for the key word "neighbor."

D   read the last paragraph.

For numbers 32 through 35, choose the best answer to the question.

32   Which of these statements makes use of a metaphor?

F   The snow was a blanket, covering the garden and burying the flowers that had just emerged from the ground.

G   The whale seemed huge, bigger than any animal Vangie had ever seen, bigger even than her house.

H   The brook made beautiful sounds, babbling over rocks and murmuring through undercut banks.

J   The hawk soared over the field, circling slowly while it watched for any movement below.

33   The river port was locked in winter's harsh grip for months.

What does this description really mean?

A   The port was locked up by the authorities.

B   The winter was colder than usual near the river.

C   Workers in the port were unfriendly in the winter.

D   The river was frozen and the port was closed.

34   Dorothea Lange was chosen by the Farm Security Administration to record the migration of people from the Great Plains to California. Her photographs were so stunning that she was recognized as one of America's foremost photographers.

This passage would most likely be found in —

F   an encyclopedia entry about migrations.

G   a biography.

H   a legend.

J   a traveler's guide to the Great Plains.

35   Which of these descriptions of an airplane trip states a fact?

A   The meal on the plane wasn't very tasty.

B   Our cabin attendant certainly seemed pleasant.

C   The plane took off almost an hour late.

D   The ride was bumpier than I expected.

STOP

Table of Contents
Language

Lesson 1   Punctuation

Examples   **Directions:** Mark the space for the punctuation mark that is needed in the sentence. Mark the space for "None" if no more punctuation marks are needed.

A   Are you sure you locked the door

    A .   **B** ,   **C** ?   **D** None

B   "You did a great job," said Ms. Harrison.

    F ?   **G** ,   **H** .   **J** None

The missing punctuation mark may be at the end of a sentence or within it. Remember to look in both places.

Look carefully at all the answer choices before you choose the one you think is correct.

Practice

1   The tree is covered with pink blossoms

    A !   **B** ?   **C** .   **D** None

2   The eagle, our national symbol, is now seen in many states.

    F ;   **G** "   **H** ,   **J** None

3   Close the umbrella before the wind blows it away

    A !   **B** ,   **C** ?   **D** None

4   Our plane landed in Texas Arizona, and California.

    F ;   **G** ,   **H** :   **J** None

5   "The store will close in fifteen minutes" announced the manager.

    A .   **B** ,   **C** ?   **D** None

6   The book you are reading *The Hobbit*, is one of my favorites.

    F ?   **G** .   **H** ,   **J** None

GO ⟩

For numbers 7-12, read each answer. Fill in the space for the choice that has a punctuation error. If there is no mistake, fill in the fourth answer space.

7 A   The principal went to the student
   B   government conference with
   C   Rita the class president.
   D   (No mistakes)

8 F   Are you going to run
   G   with us on Saturday morning.
   H   The weather is supposed to be good.
   J   (No mistakes)

9 A   "Do you think we have
   B   a chance?" asked Loni. She
   C   was getting worried about the game.
   D   (No mistakes)

10 F   823 Church St.
   G   Hanley, CA 93322
   H   April 10 1995.
   J   (No mistakes)

11 A   Dear Aunt Miriam
   B   Congratulations on your new job.
   C   I think you will be a great pilot.
   D   (No mistakes)

12 F   I can't wait to fly with you?
   G   Your nephew,
   H   Randy
   J   (No mistakes)

For numbers 13-16, read each sentence with a blank. Choose the word or words that fit best in the blank and show the correct punctuation.

13 _____ your chemistry experiment is working as we expected.

   A Cora,
   B Cora
   C Cora;
   D "Cora"

14 The carpenter will work on _____ this week.

   F the door, the windows, and the cupboards,
   G the door the windows, and the cupboards
   H the door, the windows, and the cupboards
   J the door, the windows and, the cupboards

15 The elevator is _____ we will have to wait for the next one.

   A full
   B full,
   C full:
   D full;

16 A _____ roar shattered the quiet and frightened the zebras.

   F lions
   G lion's
   H lions'
   J lions's

STOP

Examples   **Directions:** Mark the space for the answer that shows correct punctuation and capitalization. Mark the space for "Correct as it is" if the underlined part is correct.

A **A** No; you may not have any cookies.	**B** Turn the light <u>off, please.</u>
B Yes, the milk is in the refrigerator.	**F** off please
C No the fruit has not been washed yet.	**G** off, please?
D Yes; we are having a salad with dinner.	**H** off, please."
	J Correct as it is

Remember, you are looking for the answer that shows correct capitalization and punctuation.

If you are not sure which answer is correct, take your best guess.

Practice

1 **A** Our town is growing. faster than many people like.

B Have you seen the new airport. My sister says it is huge.

C The new school is already. Too small for the number of students we have.

D The new store is almost finished. It will open next week.

2 **F** Conseulo, which suitcase is yours?

G The class, returned from a trip to the Mountains.

H finally, all the bags were unpacked.

J The lodge where we stayed was in vermont.

3 **A** "What would you like to see?" Asked the guide.

B "Our business is growing quickly," commented the president.

C The engineer said "we spend a lot of time on quality control."

D Sid wanted to know, "How old the company was?"

4 The tires are <u>new but</u> the brakes still have to be fixed.

F new. But

G new but,

H new, but

J Correct as it is

5 "Meet me at the <u>restaurant suggested</u> Kim.

A restaurant," suggested

B restaurant," Suggested

C restaurant." Suggested

D Correct as it is

6 A raccoon has been raiding <u>Mr. Langford's</u> vegetable garden.

F Mr. Langfords

G Mr Langfords

H mr. Langford's

J Correct as it is

GO

ANSWER ROWS   **A** Ⓐ Ⓑ Ⓒ Ⓓ   **1** Ⓐ Ⓑ Ⓒ Ⓓ   **3** Ⓐ Ⓑ Ⓒ Ⓓ   **5** Ⓐ Ⓑ Ⓒ Ⓓ
B Ⓕ Ⓖ Ⓗ Ⓙ   **2** Ⓕ Ⓖ Ⓗ Ⓙ   **4** Ⓕ Ⓖ Ⓗ Ⓙ   **6** Ⓕ Ⓖ Ⓗ Ⓙ

61

(7)   In 1809, one of <u>America's most famous writers</u> of horror tales

(8)   <u>was born</u> Edgar Allan Poe had a special talent for writing poems

(9)   and stories that used the sounds of the <u>English Language</u> to

frighten his readers. Among his most important works are the

(10)   poem *The Raven*. <u>And the story</u> *The Pit and the Pendulum*.

---

7 **A** Americas most famous writers
   B Americas most famous writer's
   C America's most famous writer's
   D Correct as it is

8 **F** was born,
   G was. Born
   H was born.
   J Correct as it is

9 **A** English language
   B english language
   C English language,
   D Correct as it is

10 **F** *Raven*, and
   G *Raven* and
   H *raven* and
   J Correct as it is

June 20, 1995

Camp Challenge

RR 5, Box 54

(11)   <u>Afton, OH, 43561,</u>

(12)   <u>Dear Mr. Laub,</u>

Please consider me an applicant for the position of camp

(13)   <u>counselor you</u> advertised. I have enclosed a description of my

experiences and three letters of reference.

(14)   <u>Sincerely yours:</u>

Leonard Watkins

---

11 **A** afton OH, 43561
   B Afton OH 43561,
   C Afton, OH 43561
   D Correct as it is

12 **F** Dear Mr. Laub:
   G Dear Mr. Laub.
   H dear Mr. Laub:
   J Correct as it is

13 **A** Counselor you
   B Counselor, you
   C counselor you,
   D Correct as it is

14 **F** sincerely yours
   G Sincerely yours,
   H Sincerely Yours,
   J Correct as it is

GO

For numbers 15 and 16, read the sentence with a blank. Mark the space beside the answer choice that fits best in the blank and has correct capitalization and punctuation.

15 _____ will visit our school to mark the opening of the new library.

A rep Shipley
B Rep Shipley
C rep. Shipley
D Rep. Shipley

16 The storm developed in the _____ was going to be a powerful one.

F Atlantic Ocean. It
G Atlantic ocean. It
H Atlantic Ocean; It
J Atlantic Ocean, It

Parker wrote this story about two young people and their strange adventure. Read the story and use it to do numbers 17-20.

Lucia and Doug were cousins' and friends'. Their
        (1)   (2)
families took vacations together and this year they

went to the beach. It was the first morning of the
                              (3)
vacation.

"Doug, let's go for a walk on the beach" Lucia
    (4)
suggested.

"Okay," answered Doug. "Let me put my shoes on."
  (5)   (6)
Doug put his shoes on, and they started down
(7)
Ocean Avenue. They came to a dirt road that led to
            (8)
the old shipwreck.

17 In sentence 1, cousins' and friends' is best written —

A cousins and friends
B cousin's and friend's
C cousins, and friends
D As it is

18 In sentence 2, together and is best written —

F together and,
G together. And
H together, and
J As it is

19 In sentence 4, beach" Lucia is best written —

A beach," Lucia,
B beach," Lucia
C beach", Lucia
D As it is

20 In sentence 7, Ocean Avenue. is best written —

F Ocean avenue
G ocean avenue
H Ocean Avenue,
J As it is

STOP

ANSWER ROWS 15 Ⓐ Ⓑ Ⓒ Ⓓ   17 Ⓐ Ⓑ Ⓒ Ⓓ   19 Ⓐ Ⓑ Ⓒ Ⓓ
                           16 Ⓕ Ⓖ Ⓗ Ⓙ   18 Ⓕ Ⓖ Ⓗ Ⓙ   20 Ⓕ Ⓖ Ⓗ Ⓙ

Example   **Directions:** For E1 and numbers 1-4, fill in the answer circle for the punctuation mark that is needed in the sentence. If no punctuation mark is needed fill in the answer choice for "None."

E1

The computer is on the kitchen table

    A .   **B** !   **C** ?   **D** None

---

1   "That was the funniest thing I ever saw," laughed Marian.

    A "   **B** ;   **C** ?   **D** None

2   The swimming pool is open on Monday Wednesday, and Friday.

    F ;   **G** .   **H** ,   **J** None

3   Watch out, the ice is thin there

    A !   **B** ?   **C** .   **D** None

4   Your teacher, Mrs. Capelli won the marathon.

    F :   **G** ,   **H** ;   **J** None

For numbers 5-7, read each answer. Fill in the space for the choice that has a punctuation error. If there is no mistake, fill in the fourth answer space.

5   **A**   "This painting is
      B more than 400 years old,"
      C added the museum guide.
      D *(No mistakes)*

6   **F**   How do you know it is limestone.
      G It looks like every other
      H rock I have ever seen.
      J *(No mistakes)*

7   **A**   It's starting to get dark.
      B Wed better find a place
      C where we can spend the night.
      D *(No mistakes)*

For numbers 8 and 9, read each sentence with a blank. Choose the word or words that fit best in the blank and show the correct punctuation.

8   If you want to do well on the _____ study pages 54 through 78.

    F test
    G test;
    H test,
    J test.

9   The _____ we took on vacation will be developed next week.

    A pictures
    B picture's
    C pictures'
    D pictures's

GO ▷

For numbers 10-13, read each group of sentences. Find the one that is written correctly and shows the correct capitalization and punctuation.

10 F It took us several hours to drive from Orlando to fort Myers?

G Montana is West of North Dakota.

H Which is farther south, Kentucky or California.

J Wilmington, North Carolina is near the Atlantic Ocean.

11 A My Father includes bread, and a salad with every dinner he fixes.

B We had cheese, mushrooms, and onions on our pizza.

C Cereals are usually made from oats corn, and wheat.

D The plates and bowls for Dinner, are already on the table.

12 F What kinds of things do you do with your family, asked Richard.

G Marilyn answered quickly, "we go fishing almost every week."

H "One of the things we do together is hike in the park," said Janelle.

J "after dinner, we spend a few minutes practicing spanish," added Mark.

13 A The nurse is coming soon. He had to get a chart first.

B Luis is in the hospital, he hurt his foot.

C When did it happen how long will he be in the hospital?

D His mother said it isn't serious. he'll be out in a day or two.

For numbers 14-17, read the sentence with a blank. Mark the space beside the answer choice that fits best in the blank and has correct capitalization and punctuation.

14 The screen that divided the room was covered with _____

F chinese characters
G Chinese Characters.
H Chinese characters.
J Chinese characters?

15 In order to build a _____ must first get a permit from the state.

A house, you
B house. You
C house you,
D house? You

16 _____ visited our class and showed us slides of Native American ruins.

F Dr. Carlsen, and her assistant
G Dr. Carlsen and her Assistant
H Dr. Carlsen and her assistant,
J Dr. Carlsen and her assistant

17 The _____ was completed last year, but it already needs repairs.

A Bridge across the River
B bridge across the river
C bridge, across the river,
D bridge across the river,

GO

For numbers 18-21, look at the underlined part of each sentence. Find the answer choice that shows the correct capitalization and punctuation for the underlined part.

18 Toshi <u>commented we</u> should start studying for the test now."

    F commented. We

    G commented, "We

    H commented, "we

    J Correct as it is

19 The car stopped at the gas <u>station and</u> the driver asked the attendant for directions.

    A station. And

    B station and,

    C station, and

    D Correct as it is

20 The winner of the contest was from the small town of <u>Holden, Alabama.</u>

    F Holden, Alabama,

    G holden, Alabama.

    H Holden, Alabama?

    J Correct as it is

21 The truck was loaded with <u>lumber bricks,</u> and concrete for the new house.

    A lumber, bricks,

    B lumber,bricks

    C lumber, bricks.

    D Correct as it is

For numbers 22-25, read the passage. Find the answer choice that shows the correct capitalization and punctuation for the underlined part.

(22)   Historians agree that <u>millard Fillmore,</u> is the least known of

(23) the American <u>presidents born</u> in 1800, he had no formal education until he was eighteen. At that late age, he entered school and

(24) eventually became a lawyer. He entered local <u>politics was</u> elected

(25) to the <u>House of Representatives,</u> and ultimately became vice-president of the United States. Fillmore assumed the presidency when Zachary Taylor died in 1850.

22 **F** Millard Fillmore is,
    G Millard Fillmore is
    H Millard Fillmore. Is
    J Correct as it is

23 **A** presidents. Born
    B presidents, born
    C president's, born
    D Correct as it is

24 **F** politic's
    G Politics,
    H politics, was
    J Correct as it is

25 **A** house of representatives
    B House of representatives
    C House of representatives
    D Correct as it is

GO

This is more of Parker's story. Read the story and use it to do numbers 26-29.

"Let's walk down by the shipwreck," said Lucia.
(1)

"Are you sure that's a good <u>idea" answered</u> Doug.
(2)

"It's loaded with mosquitoes and it smells."
(3)

"It's windy, so there <u>wont be any bugs</u> or
(4)

smells," Lucia responded. "Don't be such a wimp."
(5)

The two of them headed down the road toward the
(6)

shipwreck. Lucia was right. There were no <u>bugs and</u>
(7)   **(8)**

it didn't smell at all. Doug was beginning to enjoy
(9)

this adventure.

The wreck they were heading toward was the
(10)

<u>remains' of</u> an old cargo ship. It had been damaged
(11)

in a storm in 1909, and the crew couldn't save it.

They all escaped, but the ship had been destroyed.
(12)

26 In sentence 2, <u>idea" answered</u> is best written —

F idea," answered
G idea?" answered
H idea" answered,"
J As it is

27 In sentence 4, <u>wont be any bugs</u> is best written —

A won't be any bugs
B won't be any bugs,
C wont' be any bugs
D As it is

28 In sentence 8, <u>bugs and</u> is best written —

F bugs. And
G bug's, and
H bugs, and
J As it is

29 In sentence 10, <u>remains' of</u> is best written —

A remains, of
B remains of
C remain's of
D As it is

67

STOP

Lesson 4   Usage

Examples   **Directions:** Read the directions for each section. Fill in the circle
for the answer you think is correct.

Which word fits best in the sentence?
A   This basketball is _____ , but she said
we could play with it.
 	
   A   hers
   B   she's
   C   her
   D   thems
	Which sentence is complete and correctly written?
	B **F** This hotel welcome families with small
	children.
	   G The parking lot close at midnight.
	   H The luggage were in the room when we
	got there.
	   J The bell rings if you press that button.

If a question is too difficult, skip it and come back to it later.

Before you mark your answer, say it to yourself. Ask yourself:
"Does this sound right?"

Practice

For numbers 1-3, choose the word or phrase
that best completes the sentence.

1   This is the _____ kitten in the litter.

   A   cuter

   B   cute

   C   cutest

   D   most cutest

2   Lucy _____ when we arrived.

   F   were painting

   G   painting

   H   was painting

   J   are painting

3   This is _____ most popular meal.

   A   our

   B   us

   C   they

   D   we

For numbers 4-6, choose the answer that is
a complete and correctly written sentence.

4   **F**   We was able to hike around the ruins
and look inside them.

   G   The students enjoyed the visitor center
at the park.

   H   The people who builded the ancient city
were talented architects.

   J   All of us buyed souvenirs from the store.

5   **A**   Me and her learned Sign Language.

   B   I and Becky helped to widen the
doorway.

   C   Holly and them will move the table.

   D   Phil and I carried the wheelchair.

6   **F**   Finding the aisle with milk and cheese.

   G   Fruits and vegetables very fresh.

   H   The cart was filled with groceries.

   J   Bread baking early in the morning.

GO

Lesson 4   Usage

For numbers 7-12, read each answer choice. Fill in the space for the choice that has a usage error. If there is no mistake, fill in the fourth answer space.

7 **A** This morning when I was walking
   B to school I saw some workers
   C built the bridge across the river.
   D *(No mistakes)*

8 **F** The elephants at the zoo
   G didn't want none of the
   H apples we tried to feed them.
   J *(No mistakes)*

9 **A** Whenever we go to a museum,
   B I visit the store and
   C buy a book or a poster.
   D *(No mistakes)*

10 **F** Ellie and Jay was waiting
   G for us in the hall. We all walked
   H to the computer lab.
   J *(No mistakes)*

11 **A** As we got closer to the lake,
   B we began to understanding why
   C so many people want to live there.
   D *(No mistakes)*

12 **F** The deer walked quieter
   G through the woods until she
   H reached the edge of the lake.
   J *(No mistakes)*

For numbers 13 and 14, choose the best way to write the underlined part of each sentence. If the underlined part is correct, fill in the fourth answer space.

13 Celina solved the puzzle by **working** slowly and carefully.

   A works
   B worked
   C work
   D *(No change)*

14 **However** the traffic was heavy, it moved quickly and we arrived on time.

   F Until
   G Although
   H Unless
   J *(No change)*

For numbers 15 and 16, choose the answer that is a complete and correctly written sentence.

15 **A** Raining heavily, Demitri wished it would stop so they could play outside.
   B Turning on the fan, the room became cool enough for Tom to study.
   C In spite of the crowd, Donna enjoyed her visit to the beach.
   D No matter what she said, the horse wouldn't follow Sheri's lead.

16 **F** The car made a funny noise when Jackson started it.
   G Cleaning up her room before Fatima went to the movies.
   H The glasses you are looking for on the table in the living room.
   J How long it takes to fly from New York to San Francisco?

GO

ANSWER ROWS   7 Ⓐ Ⓑ Ⓒ Ⓓ   9 Ⓐ Ⓑ Ⓒ Ⓓ   11 Ⓐ Ⓑ Ⓒ Ⓓ   13 Ⓐ Ⓑ Ⓒ Ⓓ   15 Ⓐ Ⓑ Ⓒ Ⓓ   **69**
8 Ⓕ Ⓖ Ⓗ Ⓙ   10 Ⓕ Ⓖ Ⓗ Ⓙ   12 Ⓕ Ⓖ Ⓗ Ⓙ   14 Ⓕ Ⓖ Ⓗ Ⓙ   16 Ⓕ Ⓖ Ⓗ Ⓙ

Here is more of Parker's story. Read the story and use it to do numbers 17-20.

It took theirselves just a few minutes to reach
(1)
the wreck. The old ship was half buried in sand at
(2)
the point where the ocean and the bay came

together. When the tide was out, you could walk to
(3)
the wreck and climb aboard.

Lucia headed for a ladder on the side of the
(4)
ship. Doug were following her slowly.
(5)
"Are you going to climb up?" asked Doug.
(6)
"Of course," answered Lucia. "That's why I
(7)   (8)
wanted to come. It's okay."
(9)
Lucia grabbed the most lowest rung and started
(10)
up the ladder. After she reached the top, Doug
(11)
started up. In a few minutes, they was standing on
(12)
the deck. It was a spooky feeling.
(13)

17 In sentence 1, theirselves is best written —

A themselves
B they
C them
D As it is

18 In sentence 5, were following is best written —

F followed
G will follow
H following
J As it is

19 In sentence 10, most lowest is best written —

A more lower
B lowest
C most lower
D As it is

20 In sentence 12, was standing is best written —

F stand
G were standing
H had stood
J As it is

STOP

Examples   Directions: For A, choose the underlined word that is the simple subject of the sentence. For B, choose the underlined word that is the predicate (verb) of the sentence. For C, choose the answer that is the best combination of the underlined sentences.

A A <u>steep</u> <u>hill</u> <u>slowed</u> the <u>climbers</u> down.
      A   B   C   D

B Two <u>large</u> <u>fish</u> <u>rested</u> under the <u>dock</u>.
      F   G   H   J

C <u>The box is blue.</u>
    <u>The box is heavy.</u>

    A The blue box is heavy.
    B The heavy blue box.
    C The box is blue but heavy.
    D The blue box, which is heavy.

 **If you are not sure which answer is correct, eliminate answers you know are wrong and then take your best guess.**

Practice

For numbers 1-3, find the underlined part that is the simple subject of the sentence.

1 <u>Our</u> <u>friends</u> met us at the <u>bowling</u> <u>alley</u>.
    A   B   C   D

2 A <u>small</u> <u>plane</u> <u>landed</u> in the <u>farmer's</u> field.
    F   G   H   J

3 <u>Two</u> <u>huge</u> <u>trees</u> stood beside the <u>entrance</u> to the park.
    A   B   C   D

For numbers 4-6, find the underlined part that is the simple predicate (verb) of the sentence.

4 <u>Mac</u> <u>found</u> a <u>turtle</u> in his <u>backyard</u>.
    F   G   H   J

5 The <u>pipes</u> to our <u>kitchen</u> <u>froze</u> <u>last</u> winter.
      A   B   C   D

6 The <u>owner</u> of the car <u>crawled</u> <u>under</u> it <u>looking</u> for the problem.
      F   G   H   J

GO

For numbers 7-9, choose the answer that best combines the underlined sentences.

7 Your cousin called this morning.

Your cousin said she will be here at noon.

  A Your cousin, calling this morning, said she will be here at noon.

  B Although she called this morning, your cousin said she will be here at noon.

  C Your cousin called this morning and said she will be here at noon.

  D This morning your cousin called, who will be here at noon.

8 The wind chimes are on the deck.

The wind chimes sound beautiful.

  F On the deck, the wind chimes sound beautiful.

  G The beautiful wind chimes sounded on the deck.

  H The wind chimes, on the deck, and sound beautiful.

  J The wind chimes on the deck sound beautiful.

9 Felicia left early.

Bruce left early.

They are going to the district debate.

  A Felicia and Bruce left early to go to the district debate.

  B Felicia and Bruce left early, although they are going to the district debate.

  C Leaving early, Felicia and Bruce, who are going to the district debate.

  D Because they are going to the district debate, so Felicia and Bruce left early.

For numbers 10 and 11, choose the best way of expressing the idea.

10 **F** Year after year in the same place, birds often nest.
    G In the same place, birds often nest year after year.
    H Birds often nest in the same place year after year.
    J Often in the same place, birds nest year after year.

11 **A** Although a water pipe was broken and repaired, workers blocked off our street.
    B Workers blocked off our street to repair a broken water pipe.
    C Our street was blocked off by workers, because to repair a broken water pipe.
    D A broken water pipe caused our street to be blocked off by workers and repaired.

72

GO

Parker's story continues here. Use the story to do numbers 12-15.

Standing on the deck were Lucia and Doug, who
(1)
had a fabulous view of the bay and the ocean. They
(2)
could see the huge ships moving up the bay and the

motorboats bouncing on the ocean waves.

Lucia looked toward the back end of the boat the
(3)
deck was damaged there and it looked like you could

see into the hold.

"Let's take a look over there," Lucia suggested.
(4)
"We might be able to see what's inside the ship."
(5)
Doug started toward the back of the boat. He
(6)   **(7)**
walked carefully. The ship was tilted and he didn't
(8)
want to fall. Lucia followed right behind him, but
(9)
stopped after a few yards.

---

12 How is sentence 1 best written?

F Standing on the deck, Lucia and Doug had a fabulous view of the bay and the ocean.

G Lucia and Doug had a fabulous view of the bay and the ocean, although standing on the deck

H While standing on the deck, a fabulous view of the bay and ocean were had by Lucia and Doug.

J As it is

13 How are sentences 7 and 8 best combined?

A He walked carefully, not wanting to fall, and the ship was tilted.

B With the ship tilted, he walked carefully, because he didn't want to fall.

C He walked carefully because the ship was tilted and he didn't want to fall.

D Because the ship was tilted, he didn't want to fall and he walked carefully.

14 Sentence 9 is best written —

F Lucia followed right behind him and stopping after a few yards.

G Stopped after a few yards, Lucia followed right behind him.

H Lucia, who had stopped after a few yards, followed right behind him.

J As it is

15 Which sentence should be broken into two sentences?

A 2
B 3
C 5
D 6

ANSWER ROWS   **12** Ⓕ Ⓖ Ⓗ Ⓙ   **13** Ⓐ Ⓑ Ⓒ Ⓓ   **14** Ⓕ Ⓖ Ⓗ Ⓙ   **15** Ⓐ Ⓑ Ⓒ Ⓓ

Example

Directions: Read the directions for each section. Fill in the circle for the answer you think is correct.

Read the paragraph below. Find the best topic sentence for the paragraph.

A _____ . Cities and states are planting wildflowers beside highways. In addition to improving the appearance of the highway, wildflowers require little maintenance. They also provide food and cover for many songbirds.

  A Highways are usually maintained by the state department of transportation.

  B Many gardeners are discovering the benefits of planting wildflowers.

  C Drivers usually don't pay much attention to the side of the road.

  D Something wonderful is happening on roadsides around America.

Stay with your first answer choice. You should change an answer only if you are sure it is incorrect.

Remember, a paragraph should focus on one idea. The correct answer is the one that fits best with the rest of the paragraph.

Practice

Read the paragraph below. Find the best topic sentence for the paragraph.

1 _____ . Water in the ground absorbs gases such as carbon dioxide. This makes the water slightly acid. Over long periods of time, the water dissolves minerals in the ground and forms caves.

  A Caves can be remarkably beautiful.

  B People who explore caves are called "spelunkers."

  C Many caves are formed by an unusual process.

  D There are many caves in the West.

Find the answer choice that best develops the topic sentence below.

2 The high-quality rubber in a car's tire is the result of an accident.

  F In 1839, Charles Goodyear dropped a mixture of hot rubber and sulfur on a stove. The rubber was greatly improved, and the tire industry was born.

  G Charles Goodyear was looking for a way to improve rubber. When it comes from the tree, it is not very useful.

  H In addition to rubber, tires are made of steel or other substances. This makes them stronger and last longer.

  J Rubber from a tree is not very useful. Many scientists were searching for the way to improve its quality.

74   **GO**

For numbers 3 and 4, read the paragraph. Find the sentence that does not belong in the paragraph.

3 1. A small island in New York harbor holds special meaning for many Americans.   2. It was the place that their ancestors first entered the United States.   3. The ships that brought them were often crowded.   4. Ellis Island, as it is known, was the entry point for millions of American immigrants.

  A Sentence 1

  B Sentence 2

  C Sentence 3

  D Sentence 4

4 1. A President of the United States has the right to name the members of the cabinet.   2. The first woman cabinet member was Frances Perkins.   3. She was named secretary of labor by President Franklin Roosevelt in 1933.   4. Perkins was also a best-selling author and a college professor.

  F Sentence 1

  G Sentence 2

  H Sentence 3

  J Sentence 4

For numbers 5 and 6, read the paragraph. Find the sentence that best fits the blank in the paragraph.

5 The G.I. Bill is often considered to be the best investment the U.S. government ever made. _____ . Because of the G.I. Bill, many veterans were able to attend college, buy a home, and receive medical care for injuries they received defending our country.

  A The government often provides money for projects to improve the life of Americans.

  B The bill was written to help millions of women and men who had been in the armed forces.

  C Colleges had to expand to handle all the new students.

  D The money for the bill was raised through taxes.

6 Homeowners are billed for their electricity by an unusual method. A standard amount of electrical current enters the house. _____ . The homeowner pays for only the current that is used.

  F Lights, a television, and other appliances run on electricity.

  G Almost everyone in the United States has electric service.

  H The electricity is usually generated many miles away.

  J Some of it is used, but the rest is returned to the electric company.

GO

For numbers 7-9, use the paragraph below to answer the questions.

> [1]He promised his little sister that he would take her to the park on Saturday. [2]Her name was Cindy, and she was eight years old. [3]Then his best friend, Andrew, called and invited him to a football game on Saturday. [4]Rufus really wanted to go to the game, but he also wanted to spend time with his sister. [5]And besides, he had made a promise to Cindy, and he always kept his promises.

7   Choose the best first sentence for this paragraph.

A Rufus was a good student in school.
B Friends and family are important, as Rufus would find out.
C Rufus wasn't sure what to do.
D Many young people don't have much to do on the weekend.

8   Which sentence should be left out of this paragraph?

F Sentence 1
G Sentence 2
H Sentence 4
J Sentence 5

9   Choose the best last sentence for this paragraph.

A Making decisions was something Rufus didn't do well, so he went to the library to get a book about football.
B Most people would be happy to have such good choices.
C The park was near his home, but the football stadium was far away.
D He sat on the porch and stared out into the street, hoping the answer would come to him.

10   Which of the following would be most appropriate in a letter asking for permission to have a bake sale in front of a store?

F The students in our class are raising money for a computer and software. We would like your permission to set up a table on Saturday and sell baked goods in front of your store. We promise to clean up when we are finished and not to bother your customers.

G Your store is one of the nicest ones on Main Street. Many people come by, especially on Saturday. We would like to set up a table then and sell baked goods. Because so many people come by, we will probably make a lot of money.

H Our class has 27 students. The teacher's name is Mr. Boynton. We think he is one of the best teachers in the school. Mr. Boynton got us all interested in computers. Now we would like to have one in our classroom and need money to buy it.

J The students in our class think the best place to raise money is in front of your store. We need a computer for our class. No one will give us the money. We want to sell baked goods on Saturday, and we will set up our table from 9:00 in the morning until 4:00 in the afternoon.

Here is more of Parker's story about Lucia and Doug. Use the story to do numbers 11-14.

"Doug, did you hear that?"
(1)
"No, what did it sound like?" Doug walked back
(2)   **(3)**
toward Lucia.

"I can't describe the sound very well. It was
(4)   **(5)**
kind of like a squeak, but real soft."

There wasn't enough light to see well, but they
(6)
heard the noise again. Suddenly they both knew what
(7)
the sound was. They were hearing kittens!
(8)
"Some kittens must be stuck here. How on earth
(9)   **(10)**
did they get here? What are we going to do?" asked
(11)
Doug. He had never had a kitten himself.
(12)
"The mother cat must be around somewhere.
(13)
Kittens don't just <u>show up</u>. We shouldn't do
(14)   **(15)**
anything until we find out where the mother is.

This is a very strange place to stumble onto a
(16)
bunch of kittens," Lucia answered.

---

11 **Which sentence could be added after sentence 16?**

A "Be careful when you are walking."
B "Let's look around for the mother."
C "How did this hole get here?"
D "I wonder what kind of kittens they are?"

12 **Which sentence could begin the fourth paragraph?**

F The ship was in pretty good shape for being so old.
G Doug looked out over the bay.
H Strange things happen on old ships.
J The two of them looked into a hole in the deck of the ship.

13 **Which group of words would be more colorful than the underlined words in sentence 14?**

A appear out of nowhere
B come on ships
C hide in the dark
D make noises in the dark

14 **Which sentence does *not* belong in the story?**

F 2
G 5
H 12
J 15

STOP

Lesson 7   Test Yourself

Example   Directions: Find the underlined part that is the simple predicate (verb) of the sentence.

E1

Find the underlined part that is the simple predicate (verb) of the sentence.

The <u>driver</u> of the <u>truck</u> <u>stopped</u> for <u>fuel</u>.
    A   B   C   D

For number 1, choose the word or phrase that best completes the sentence.

1   Next Tuesday we _____ for the student council members in our school.

  A voted

  B will vote

  C have voted

  D were voting

For number 2, choose the answer that is a complete and correctly written sentence.

2   **F** The meal you cooked for them was just wonderful.

  G Theirs went shopping for vegetables and meat at the supermarket.

  H One of the workers helped she grandmother load the car.

  J Please pass the bread and the salad to he.

For numbers 3-5, read each answer choice. Fill in the space for the choice that has a usage error. If there is no mistake, fill in the fourth answer space.

3   **A** The desk you bought looks
  B beautiful. Where do you think
  C you will put it in your room?
  D *(No mistakes)*

4   **F** We'll never get this
  G homework done on time.
  H We shoulda gone to the library.
  J *(No mistakes)*

5   **A** The batteries you bought
  B don't never last more
  C than a week or two.
  D *(No mistakes)*

For number 6, find the underlined part that is the simple subject of the sentence.

6   <u>Planes</u> <u>land</u> at the <u>airport</u> about every three <u>minutes</u>.
   F   G   H   J

For number 7, find the underlined part that is the simple predicate (verb) of the sentence.

7   A <u>successful</u> business <u>owner</u> <u>spoke</u> at our <u>school</u> last week.
     A   B C   D

GO

ANSWER ROWS   **E1** Ⓐ Ⓑ Ⓒ Ⓓ   **2** Ⓕ Ⓖ Ⓗ Ⓙ   **4** Ⓕ Ⓖ Ⓗ Ⓙ   **6** Ⓕ Ⓖ Ⓗ Ⓙ

78   **1** Ⓐ Ⓑ Ⓒ Ⓓ   **3** Ⓐ Ⓑ Ⓒ Ⓓ   **5** Ⓐ Ⓑ Ⓒ Ⓓ   **7** Ⓐ Ⓑ Ⓒ Ⓓ

For numbers 8-10, choose the answer that best combines the underlined sentences.

8 Brian is carrying a large box.

His brother is helping him.

  F Brian is helping his brother, who is carrying a large box.
  G A large box is being carried by Brian, who is being helped by his brother.
  H Brian is carrying a large box, and his brother is helping him.
  J Brian is being helped to carry a large box by his brother.

9 Please turn on the fan.

The fan is in the living room.

  A Please turn on the fan, the fan that is in the living room.
  B Please turn on the fan in the living room.
  C The fan that is in the living room, please turn it on.
  D In the living room is the fan that you should turn on.

10 Ms. Baker enjoys jogging.

She jogs every day.

She jogs at four o'clock.

  F Ms. Baker enjoys jogging, and she jogs every day at four o'clock.
  G At four o'clock, Ms. Baker enjoys jogging every day.
  H Jogging every day at four o'clock, Ms. Baker enjoys it.
  J Ms. Baker enjoys jogging every day at four o'clock.

For numbers 11 and 12, choose the best way of expressing the idea.

11 **A** In the living room is a picture, and it was painted by my grandmother's friend.
  B The picture in the living room was painted by my grandmother's friend.
  C It was my grandmother's friend whose picture was painted in the living room.
  D In the living room, my grandmother's friend, who painted a picture.

12 **F** The police officer said the road was closed, so we had to go another way.
  G We had to go another way, and the police officer said the road was closed.
  H Because the police officer said the road was closed, and we had to go another way.
  J Although the police officer said the road was closed, we had to go another way.

GO

Read the paragraph below. Find the best topic sentence for the paragraph.

13 _____ . Oil allows engine parts to move smoothly and protects them against moisture. After a few thousand miles, however, oil becomes sticky and dirty. It is a good idea to change the oil in a car about every 3000 miles.

   A Changing the oil in a car is one of the most important maintenance steps.

   B The oil you put in a car was probably found deep under ground.

   C Like other mechanical devices, cars require routine maintenance.

   D Oil has been used in many ways for thousands of years.

Find the answer choice that best develops the topic sentence.

14 The Colorado River is a truly amazing resource.

   F It begins as a small stream in Colorado. The river grows as other rivers join it as the Colorado makes its way to the Gulf of California.

   G Dams have created several huge lakes on the Colorado River. The Grand Canyon was also created by the Colorado River.

   H In some places, you can walk across it easily. In others, the Colorado is huge and powerful.

   J It provides drinking water and electric power to millions of people in the West. In addition, the Colorado River offers great boating and fishing.

Read the paragraph below. Find the sentence that does not belong in the paragraph.

15 1. The scaled quail makes its home in Mexico and the American Southwest.   2. It rarely rains in this region of the world.   3. It's distinctive feature is a topknot of white, cottony feathers.   4. This feature gives the scaled quail its most common name, "cotton top."

   A Sentence 1

   B Sentence 2

   C Sentence 3

   D Sentence 4

Read the paragraph below. Find the sentence that best fits the blank in the paragraph.

16   Many people have discovered an interesting hobby. They have connected a computer to a special type of radio. _____. These pictures are the same as those used by meteorologists to predict the weather.

   F Amateur radio enthusiasts are known as "hams."

   G The connection can be made easily with standard cables.

   H With this setup, they can receive pictures of the earth from satellites.

   J One type of satellite is called a Low Earth Orbiting satellite or "LEO."

GO

ANSWER ROW   **13** Ⓐ Ⓑ Ⓒ Ⓓ   **14** Ⓕ Ⓖ Ⓗ Ⓙ   **15** Ⓐ Ⓑ Ⓒ Ⓓ   **16** Ⓕ Ⓖ Ⓗ Ⓙ

Below is more of Parker's story about the mysterious kittens. Read the story and use it to do numbers 17-20.

Lucia and Doug walked carefully around the deck
(1)
of the ship. There were so many places for a cat to
(2)
hide they didn't know where to begin.

They were heading back to the hole when Lucia
(3)
whispered, "Look, Doug, a cat is walking on the

beach. Be quiet and <u>lets see, what</u> it does."
(4)
The cat walked up the beach with a mouse in her
(5)
mouth. Because the tide was so low, she could come
(6)
right up to the ship and jump in through a hole. In
(7)
a few seconds, the kittens making even more noise.

"That's the end of the mystery, Doug," said
(8)
Lucia. Let's get off this ship before the tide
(9)
comes in. I can't wait to tell everybody how we
(10)
solved the kitten mystery."

17 **Which sentence could be added after sentence 2?**

A   Suddenly, the tide began to come in.
B   They decided to walk back to where they first heard the kittens.
C   The ship was very big.
D   This was one time they wished they had a radio.

18 **How is sentence 5 best written?**

F   Walking up the beach, the cat with a mouse in her mouth.
G   On the beach was a cat, walking up the beach, and with a mouse in her mouth.
H   The cat, which walked up the beach, with a mouse in her mouth.
J   As it is

19 **Which group of words is not a complete thought?**

A   2
B   6
C   7
D   10

20 **In sentence 4, <u>lets see, what</u> is best written —**

F   let's see what
G   let's see. What
H   lets see what,
J   As it is

81

STOP

Lesson 8   Spelling Skills

Examples   **Directions:** Follow the directions for each section. Choose the answer you think is correct.

Find the word that is spelled correctly and fits best in the sentence.	One of the underlined words is misspelled. Which answer choice is incorrect?
A Have you finished your _____?	B F feel <u>contented</u>
A drawrring	G <u>never</u> find
B drawing	H <u>levul</u> field
C draweng	J great <u>wisdom</u>
D drawng	

 **Tips**   Read the directions carefully. Be sure you know if you should look for the correctly spelled word or the incorrectly spelled word.

As soon as you know which answer is correct, mark it and move on to the next item.

Practice

For numbers 1-5, find the word that is spelled correctly and fits best in the blank.

1 What is that _____ in the jar?

   A   liqid
   B   liquid
   C   liqued
   D   liguid

2 Each member of the band wears a _____.

   F   unaform
   G   uniferm
   H   uniform
   J   unifrom

3 The _____ had many unusual fish.

   A   aguarium
   B   aquareum
   C   aqarium
   D   aquarium

4 Our family has many _____.

   F   triditions
   G   traditions
   H   tradations
   J   tradetions

5 The _____ city was built on top of a hill.

   A   ancient
   B   anchient
   C   anchint
   D   aincient

For numbers 6-8, read the phrases. Choose the phrase in which the underlined word is **not** spelled correctly.

6 F   <u>exact</u> change

   G   <u>sourse</u> of water

   H   clam <u>shell</u>

   J   always <u>disagree</u>

7 A   <u>place</u> a package

   B   right <u>verdict</u>

   C   fishing <u>tackle</u>

   D   <u>barder</u> for goods

8 F   leave <u>earlyer</u>

   G   <u>block</u> a street

   H   move <u>forward</u>

   J   find a <u>quarter</u>

GO ▷

For numbers 9-11, read each answer. Fill in the space for the choice that has a spelling error. If there is no mistake, fill in the last answer space.

9 A evidince
   B produce
   C weld
   D attend
   E *(No mistakes)*

10 F bright
   G term
   H playful
   J employ
   K *(No mistakes)*

11 A fable
   B building
   C crust
   D nonsence
   E *(No mistakes)*

For numbers 12-14, read each phrase. One of the underlined words is not spelled correctly for the way it is used in the phrase. Fill in the space for the word that is not spelled correctly.

12 F turn quickly
   G get dirty
   H except an offer
   J school motto

13 A police officer
   B dog's pause
   C recall a name
   D tasty fruit

14 F huge rock
   G good idea
   H four daze
   J spool of thread

For numbers 15-18, find the underlined part that is misspelled. If all the words are spelled correctly, mark the space under <u>No mistake</u>.

15 What is the averige length of the fish you caught? No mistake.
          A   B   C   D

16 We must decide what the title of our essay will be. No mistake.
            F   G   H   J

17 Our company will pravide you with the materials you need to repair the leak. No mistake.
         A   B   C   D

18 We tried to convinse Shirley that my pet snake was not dangerous. No mistake.
        F   G   H   J

Lesson 9   Test Yourself

Examples   Directions: For E1, find the word that shows the correct spelling and fits best in the sentence. For E2, look for the underlined word that has a spelling mistake. Mark your answer.

E1

Noreen solved a _____ problem.

A cumplex
B complix
C complecks
D complex

E2

F ajust the volume
G nearly empty
H write an outline
J large poster

For numbers 1-6, find the word that is spelled correctly and fits best in the blank.

1 Today's _____ may be gone tomorrow.

A fashion
B fashen
C fashun
D fation

2 I _____ you the diamond is real.

F asure
G assure
H assuer
J asuer

3 Did you _____ the dog's owner?

A lowcate
B loacate
C locate
D locait

4 The _____ of that house is Mr. Brown.

F ocupant
G occuppant
H occupant
J occupent

5 The cat was _____ about the box.

A curious
B curyous
C cureous
D cureious

6 Hard work can overcome a _____ .

F chalenge
G challange
H challunge
J challenge

For numbers 7-10, read the phrases. Choose the phrase in which the underlined word is not spelled correctly.

7 A follow the trail
B build an enclozure
C ask a question
D second choice

8 F small stream
G return the book
H indacate the answer
J rarely visit

9 A messy room
B enstruct me
C deep harbor
D beautiful island

10 F refuse to go
G leave without
H suggest an answer
J want to persue

GO

For numbers 11-13, read each answer. Fill in the space for the choice that has a spelling error. If there is no mistake, fill in the last answer space.

11 A answer
    B relutive
    C continue
    D feared
    E (No mistakes)

12 F lengthen
    G button
    H apartament
    J measure
    K (No mistakes)

13 A multaply
    B proper
    C trash
    D establish
    E (No mistakes)

For numbers 14-16, read each phrase. One of the underlined words is not spelled correctly for the way it is used in the phrase. Fill in the space for the word that is not spelled correctly.

14 F strong belief
    G difficult job
    H tide a knot
    J pardon me

15 A repeat a song
    B as usual
    C electric drill
    D here a sound

16 F busy rowed
    G attract birds
    H almost fainted
    J hide and seek

For numbers 17-20, find the underlined part that is misspelled. If all the words are spelled correctly, mark the space under No mistake.

17 Did you notise that the train station has been painted? No mistake.
         A   B   C   D

18 The change of seasons from fall to winter was gradual. No mistake.
         F   G   H   J

19 It took almost two hours to assembel the bicycle. No mistake.
            A   B   C   D

20 We were suposed to travel to Idaho tomorrow. No mistake.
            F   G   H   J

ANSWER ROWS   11 Ⓐ Ⓑ Ⓒ Ⓓ Ⓔ   14 Ⓕ Ⓖ Ⓗ Ⓙ Ⓚ   17 Ⓐ Ⓑ Ⓒ Ⓓ Ⓔ   19 Ⓐ Ⓑ Ⓒ Ⓓ Ⓔ
              12 Ⓕ Ⓖ Ⓗ Ⓙ Ⓚ   15 Ⓐ Ⓑ Ⓒ Ⓓ Ⓔ   18 Ⓕ Ⓖ Ⓗ Ⓙ Ⓚ   20 Ⓕ Ⓖ Ⓗ Ⓙ Ⓚ
              13 Ⓐ Ⓑ Ⓒ Ⓓ Ⓔ   16 Ⓕ Ⓖ Ⓗ Ⓙ Ⓚ   NUMBER RIGHT _____

Example   **Directions:** Follow the directions for each section. Choose the answer you think is correct.

Table of Contents

Chapter		Page
1	The First Colleges	1
2	Colleges in America	15
3	College Life Today	24
4	Choosing a College	30

A If you wanted to find out what it is like to be a college student, you should look on—

A pages 1-5
B pages 5-14
C pages 24-29
D pages 30 -35

 **Tips**   Remember, if you are not sure which answer is correct, eliminate choices you know are wrong and then take your best guess.

Practice

The illustration below shows a set of encyclopedias. Each of the numbered volumes holds information about topics that begin with the letters shown on that volume. Use the picture to do numbers 1 and 2.

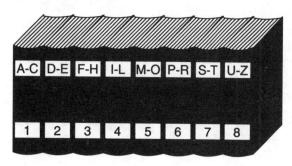

Use this part of a page from a telephone book to answer numbers 3 and 4.

Martinez, Carlos	12 Ranch St.	867-0653
Massey, Adrian	5669 Aston La.	889-1937
Meckles, Stan	287 Main St.	867-2244
Miller, Sarah	110 Laurel St.	843-9098
Milutsky, Ray	5752 Aston La.	889-4179
Morgan, Jefferson	8 River Ter.	843-0826

1 Which volume would tell you how to find the number of calories in different foods?

A Volume 1
B Volume 3
C Volume 5
D Volume 8

2 Which volume might have information about baseball, football, and ice hockey?

F Volume 1   H Volume 4
G Volume 3   J Volume 7

3 Where does Sarah Miller live?

A 5669 Aston La.
B 287 Main St.
C 110 Laurel St.
D 12 Ranch St.

4 Ray Milutsky lives very near—

F Jefferson Morgan
G Carlos Martinez
H Adrian Massey
J Stan Meckles

GO

ANSWER ROWS   A Ⓐ Ⓑ Ⓒ Ⓓ   1 Ⓐ Ⓑ Ⓒ Ⓓ   2 Ⓕ Ⓖ Ⓗ Ⓙ   3 Ⓐ Ⓑ Ⓒ Ⓓ   4 Ⓕ Ⓖ Ⓗ Ⓙ

Use this card from a library card catalog to do numbers 5-8.

622.4

ALTHEA GIBSON

922   Kennedy, Thomas
T665   The Lady Came to Play / by Thomas
        Kennedy. Photographs by Sports
        Archives. Chicago: Sanderson
        Publishing Company, 1995.
        256 p.; photos; 24 cm

        1. Gibson, Althea   2. Athletes, African-
        American   3. Athletes, female   I. Title

5 From this library catalog card, you know that Althea Gibson is—

A the author
B the publisher
C a singer
D an athlete

6 What is the title of this book?

F Althea Gibson
G The Lady Came to Play
H Thomas Kennedy
J Kennedy, Thomas

7 In which section of the card catalog would this card be found?

A Title
B Subject
C Publisher
D Author

8 Where did the photographs for this book come from?

F Sanderson Publishing Company
G Althea Gibson
H Sports Archives
J Thomas Kennedy

Read each question below. Mark the space for the answer you think is correct.

9 Look at these guide words from a dictionary page.

chimp–cholla

Which word could be found on the page?

A chin   **C** chore
B chime   **D** chief

10 Look at these guide words from a dictionary page.

aroma–arrange

Which word could be found on the page?

F arid   **H** artist
G arsenic   **J** around

11 Which of these is a main heading that includes the other three words?

A Tuesday
B Friday
C Day
D Saturday

12 Which of these is a main heading that includes the other three words?

F Ocean
G Pond
H River
J Water

13 If these words were organized from largest to smallest, which would be first?

A Table
B Dish
C Kitchen
D House

ANSWER ROWS   **5** Ⓐ Ⓑ Ⓒ Ⓓ   **7** Ⓐ Ⓑ Ⓒ Ⓓ   **9** Ⓐ Ⓑ Ⓒ Ⓓ   **11** Ⓐ Ⓑ Ⓒ Ⓓ   **13** Ⓐ Ⓑ Ⓒ Ⓓ   87
               6 Ⓕ Ⓖ Ⓗ Ⓙ   **8** Ⓕ Ⓖ Ⓗ Ⓙ   **10** Ⓕ Ⓖ Ⓗ Ⓙ   **12** Ⓕ Ⓖ Ⓗ Ⓙ

Examples   Directions: Read each question. Mark the answer that you think is correct.

E1	E2
Where could you find out how to break the word *computers* into syllables? A a dictionary B an encyclopedia C an atlas D an almanac	Which of these would probably appear in the index of a book about computers? F *Thinking Machines* by Ann Martin G CPU: central processing unit H supercomputers, 346-355 J Chapter 2, "The Electronic Brain"

Natasha is writing a report about computers. She began by making the web below. Use it to do numbers 1-4.

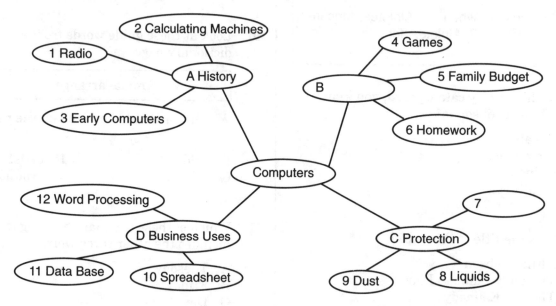

1   Which of these should go in circle B?

    A Engineering
    B Home Uses
    C Manufacturing
    D Education Uses

3   Which of these belongs in circle 7?

    A Keyboards
    B Room Size
    C Learning about Computers
    D Lightning

2   Which idea in Natasha's web does *not* belong?

    F 1
    G 4
    H 6
    J 12

4   If Natasha wanted to add a circle E to the web, which of these would be best?

    F Education Uses
    G Television
    H Recipes
    J Banking

GO

Study this table about civilizations in Mexico and Central America. Then do numbers 5-8.

Location	Civilization	Year
Central Mexico	Tenochtitlan	1500
	Cacaxtla	800
Oaxaca	Mitla	900
	Monte Alban II	200
Gulf Coast	Aztec	1300
	Huastec	1100
West Mexico	Tarascan	1450
	Ixtlan	300
Lowland Maya	Palenque	600
	Chichen Itza	1000

5 Which of these civilizations was the earliest?

   A Monte Alban II
   B Chichen Itza
   C Tarascan
   D Tenochtitlan

6 When was Chichen Itza in existence?

   F 200
   G 300
   H 600
   J 1000

7 Which of these civilizations was found on the Gulf Coast?

   A Mitla
   B Palenque
   C Aztec
   D Cacaxtla

8 Imagine that you are a time traveler and visited West Mexico around the year 300. Which civilization would you encounter?

   F Mitla
   G Ixtlan
   H Aztec
   J Palenque

For numbers 9-11, choose the word that would appear first if the words were arranged in alphabetical order.

9 A native
    B natural
    C nation
    D natty

10 F center
     G century
     H central
     J cent

11 A Stevens, Janna
     B Stevens, Karl
     C Stevens, Kenneth
     D Stevens, Jennifer

For numbers 12 and 13, choose the best source of information.

12 Which of these would tell you the names of the rivers in Canada?

   F an atlas
   G a dictionary
   H a thesaurus
   J a book of quotations

13 Which of these would help you decide what kinds of plants would do best in a shady area beside your house?

   A a book about building decks and patios on an existing home
   B an encyclopedia
   C a gardening book
   D a book about astronomy and the motion of the sun

GO

Use the Table of Contents and Index below to answer numbers 14-18. They are from a book about geology.

Table of Contents

Index

14 In which chapter would you probably find information about gold mines in ancient South America?

F Chapter 1
G Chapter 5
H Chapter 7
J Chapter 8

15 Look at the index and then the table of contents. What can you conclude about fluorite?

A It is a rock or mineral.
B It is mined.
C It is a type of fossil.
D It is caused by erosion.

16 On which page would you be most likely to find information about the past movement of the continents?

F Page 94
G Page 68
H Page 51
J Page 23

17 Which of these topics is found in Chapter 4?

A borax
B frost
C dinosaurs
D fool's gold

18 From looking at the index, what can you conclude about geologic dating?

F It is used in determining where oil and gas are found.
G It is based on fossil fish.
H There are at least two methods of determining geologic dates.
J There is a relationship between calderas and geologic dating.

To the Student:

These tests will give you a chance to put the tips you have learned to work.

A few last reminders…

- Be sure you understand all the directions before you begin each test. You may ask the teacher questions about the directions if you do not understand them.
- Work as quickly as you can during each test.
- When you change an answer, be sure to erase your first mark completely.

- You can guess at an answer or skip difficult items and go back to them later.
- Use the tips you have learned whenever you can.
- It is OK to be a little nervous. You may even do better.

Now that you have completed the lessons in this unit, you are on your way to scoring high!

STUDENT'S NAME			SCHOOL
LAST	FIRST	MI	TEACHER

FEMALE ◯   MALE ◯

BIRTHDATE

MONTH	DAY	YEAR

JAN ◯   FEB ◯   MAR ◯   APR ◯   MAY ◯   JUN ◯   JUL ◯   AUG ◯   SEP ◯   OCT ◯   NOV ◯   DEC ◯

GRADE
⑤   ⑥   ⑦

PART 1 LANGUAGE MECHANICS

E1 Ⓐ Ⓑ Ⓒ Ⓓ	**4** Ⓕ Ⓖ Ⓗ Ⓙ	**8** Ⓕ Ⓖ Ⓗ Ⓙ	**12** Ⓕ Ⓖ Ⓗ Ⓙ	**16** Ⓕ Ⓖ Ⓗ Ⓙ	**19** Ⓐ Ⓑ Ⓒ Ⓓ
1 Ⓐ Ⓑ Ⓒ Ⓓ	**5** Ⓐ Ⓑ Ⓒ Ⓓ	**9** Ⓐ Ⓑ Ⓒ Ⓓ	**13** Ⓐ Ⓑ Ⓒ Ⓓ	**17** Ⓐ Ⓑ Ⓒ Ⓓ	**20** Ⓕ Ⓖ Ⓗ Ⓙ
2 Ⓕ Ⓖ Ⓗ Ⓙ	**6** Ⓕ Ⓖ Ⓗ Ⓙ	**10** Ⓕ Ⓖ Ⓗ Ⓙ	**14** Ⓕ Ⓖ Ⓗ Ⓙ	**18** Ⓕ Ⓖ Ⓗ Ⓙ	**21** Ⓐ Ⓑ Ⓒ Ⓓ
3 Ⓐ Ⓑ Ⓒ Ⓓ	**7** Ⓐ Ⓑ Ⓒ Ⓓ	**11** Ⓐ Ⓑ Ⓒ Ⓓ	**15** Ⓐ Ⓑ Ⓒ Ⓓ		

PART 2 LANGUAGE EXPRESSION

E1 Ⓐ Ⓑ Ⓒ Ⓓ	**4** Ⓕ Ⓖ Ⓗ Ⓙ	**8** Ⓕ Ⓖ Ⓗ Ⓙ	**12** Ⓕ Ⓖ Ⓗ Ⓙ	**15** Ⓐ Ⓑ Ⓒ Ⓓ	**18** Ⓕ Ⓖ Ⓗ Ⓙ
1 Ⓐ Ⓑ Ⓒ Ⓓ	**5** Ⓐ Ⓑ Ⓒ Ⓓ	**9** Ⓐ Ⓑ Ⓒ Ⓓ	**13** Ⓐ Ⓑ Ⓒ Ⓓ	**16** Ⓕ Ⓖ Ⓗ Ⓙ	**19** Ⓐ Ⓑ Ⓒ Ⓓ
2 Ⓕ Ⓖ Ⓗ Ⓙ	**6** Ⓕ Ⓖ Ⓗ Ⓙ	**10** Ⓕ Ⓖ Ⓗ Ⓙ	**14** Ⓕ Ⓖ Ⓗ Ⓙ	**17** Ⓐ Ⓑ Ⓒ Ⓓ	**20** Ⓕ Ⓖ Ⓗ Ⓙ
3 Ⓐ Ⓑ Ⓒ Ⓓ	**7** Ⓐ Ⓑ Ⓒ Ⓓ	**11** Ⓐ Ⓑ Ⓒ Ⓓ			

PART 3 SPELLING

E1 Ⓐ Ⓑ Ⓒ Ⓓ	**3** Ⓐ Ⓑ Ⓒ Ⓓ	**7** Ⓐ Ⓑ Ⓒ Ⓓ	**11** Ⓐ Ⓑ Ⓒ Ⓓ Ⓔ	**15** Ⓐ Ⓑ Ⓒ Ⓓ	**19** Ⓐ Ⓑ Ⓒ Ⓓ
E2 Ⓕ Ⓖ Ⓗ Ⓙ	**4** Ⓕ Ⓖ Ⓗ Ⓙ	**8** Ⓕ Ⓖ Ⓗ Ⓙ	**12** Ⓕ Ⓖ Ⓗ Ⓙ Ⓚ	**16** Ⓕ Ⓖ Ⓗ Ⓙ	**20** Ⓕ Ⓖ Ⓗ Ⓙ
1 Ⓐ Ⓑ Ⓒ Ⓓ	**5** Ⓐ Ⓑ Ⓒ Ⓓ	**9** Ⓐ Ⓑ Ⓒ Ⓓ	**13** Ⓐ Ⓑ Ⓒ Ⓓ Ⓔ	**17** Ⓐ Ⓑ Ⓒ Ⓓ	
2 Ⓕ Ⓖ Ⓗ Ⓙ	**6** Ⓕ Ⓖ Ⓗ Ⓙ	**10** Ⓕ Ⓖ Ⓗ Ⓙ	**14** Ⓕ Ⓖ Ⓗ Ⓙ	**18** Ⓕ Ⓖ Ⓗ Ⓙ	

PART 4 STUDY SKILLS

E1 Ⓐ Ⓑ Ⓒ Ⓓ	**3** Ⓐ Ⓑ Ⓒ Ⓓ	**6** Ⓕ Ⓖ Ⓗ Ⓙ	**9** Ⓐ Ⓑ Ⓒ Ⓓ
1 Ⓐ Ⓑ Ⓒ Ⓓ	**4** Ⓕ Ⓖ Ⓗ Ⓙ	**7** Ⓐ Ⓑ Ⓒ Ⓓ	**10** Ⓕ Ⓖ Ⓗ Ⓙ
2 Ⓕ Ⓖ Ⓗ Ⓙ	**5** Ⓐ Ⓑ Ⓒ Ⓓ	**8** Ⓕ Ⓖ Ⓗ Ⓙ	

UNIT 5   TEST PRACTICE

Part 1   Language Mechanics

Example   **Directions:** Fill in the circle for the punctuation that is needed in the sentence. Choose "None" if no more punctuation is needed.

E1

"The elevator is too slow," muttered Jerome.

A .   **B** !   **C** ?   **D** None

---

1   Chicago Baltimore, and Philadelphia are all shipping centers.

A :   **B** ,   **C** ;   **D** None

2   "How will we know when the bread is done" asked Niki.

F ?   **G** ,   **H** !   **J** None

3   It is up to you Arlo, to decide if this job is for you.

A "   **B** ,   **C** "   **D** None

4   It took us about fifteen minutes to clean up after dinner.

F ,   **G** ?   **H** :   **J** None

For numbers 5-7, read each answer. Fill in the space for the choice that has a punctuation error. If there is no mistake, fill in the fourth answer space.

5   **A**   Learn to shop wisely.
    B   It will save you money,
    C   especially on expensive items.
    D   *(No mistakes)*

6   **F**   The bus stopped suddenly
    G   A fire truck came up the road
    H   and passed by quickly.
    J   *(No mistakes)*

7   **A**   Joe has an interview on
    B   Monday at two o'clock with
    C   Sondra the owner of the store.
    D   *(No mistakes)*

For numbers 8 and 9, read each sentence with a blank. Choose the word or words that fit best in the blank and show the correct punctuation.

8   The neighbors will be away next_____ and we will keep an eye on their house.

    F   week
    G   week,
    H   week.
    J   week:

9   The _____ of a plant absorb moisture from the soil.

    A   root's
    B   roots'
    C   roots
    D   roots's

For numbers 10-13, read each group of sentences. Find the one that is written correctly and shows the correct capitalization and punctuation.

10 F   The students in Mr. Sanders class have very interesting background's.

    G   Jonathan, a native american, is from the Southwest corner of Colorado

    H   In 1945, Hafir's grandparents arrived in New York.

    J   The class president, Sam is from the african country of Liberia.

11 A   Owning a pet can be fun. It is also a great responsibility?

    B   The shelter has many kinds of pets. it is sometimes hard to choose one

    C   feeding a pet is part of the job? There are many other things to do.

    D   Which puppy is yours? They all look so much alike.

12 F   What do you like best about your new car, asked Jorge?

    G   "It's big and comfortable but gets good gas mileage," answered Bonnie.

    H   Allie asked, When will we all get to ride in it?"

    J   Yes, added Marcellus. "It looks like it could hold all of us"

13 A   If you rest now, Nadine, you will finish the job more easily.

    B   Ms. Tingley what is a good exercise to build arm strength.

    C   Does anyone know where alonzo dropped his shoes.

    D   The Weights you are holding, Liza are just about right for you.

For numbers 14-16, read the sentence with a blank. Mark the space beside the answer choice that fits best in the blank and has correct capitalization and punctuation.

14 A _____ were on the counter.

    F   quarter and two dimes
    G   quarter, and two dimes,
    H   Quarter, and two Dimes,
    J   Quarter and two Dimes

15 _____ is just a few blocks from my grandmother's house.

    A   The pacific ocean
    B   The Pacific ocean,
    C   The Pacific Ocean
    D   The Pacific ocean;

16 The train is _____ we wait or go home and come back?

    F   late, should
    G   late? Should
    H   late, Should
    J   late. Should

Choose the correct answer for number 17.

17 Which is the correct way to end a letter?

    A   Your Friend
    B   Your friend:
    C   Your friend,
    D   Your Friend:

GO

Giselle is writing a report on gardening for a class assignment. Read the report and use it to do numbers 18-21.

> The most popular active pastime in <u>the world</u>
> **(1)**
> isn't fishing or soccer, collecting or jogging. It
> **(2)**
> is gardening, and it is enjoyed by billions of
>
> people. From the <u>Northernmost regions</u> of
> **(3)**
> Scandinavia to tropical Africa, gardens appear as
>
> if by magic anyplace where there is soil and
>
> sunshine.
>
>   Gardens can be broadly grouped into two
>   **(4)**
> categories. Ornamental gardens of <u>flowers grasses</u>,
>   **(5)**
> and other plants are meant to please the senses.
>
> Vegetable and fruit gardens are mainly intended to
> **(6)**
> provide <u>food but</u> they can also be attractive. Most
>   **(7)**
> people who consider themselves serious gardeners
>
> usually have both kinds.

18 In sentence 1, <u>the world</u> is best written —

F the World
G The World
H the World,
J As it is

19 In sentence 3, <u>Northernmost regions</u> is best written —

A northernmost regions,
B northernmost regions
C Northernmost Regions
D As it is

20 In sentence 5, <u>flowers grasses</u> is best written —

F flowers, grasses
G flowers. Grasses
H flowers; grasses
J As it is

21 In sentence 6, <u>food but</u> is best written —

A food but,
B food. But
C food, but
D As it is

STOP

Example   Directions: Find the underlined part that is the simple predicate (verb) of the sentence.

E1

A <u>full</u> <u>pitcher</u> of milk <u>fell</u> from the <u>table</u>.

  A   B   C   D

For number 1, choose the word or phrase that best completes the sentence.

1 It has been raining _____ for more than three days.

   A heavy

   B heavier

   C heavily

   D heaviest

For number 2, choose the answer that is a complete and correctly written sentence.

2 F My family taking a different kind of vacation each year.

   G We spent a week of our vacation in Virginia last summer.

   H My favorite camping in the woods or at the beach.

   J One year our vacation in New York and a play each night.

For numbers 3-5, read each answer choice. Fill in the space for the choice that has a usage error. If there is no mistake, fill in the fourth answer space.

3 A Cindy arrived early and
   B didn't give me no time
   C to get all of my clothes packed.
   D *(No mistakes)*

4 F The largest of the elephants
   G are very friendly and enjoy
   H playing with their keepers.
   J *(No mistakes)*

5 A The parking space was so
   B tiny that I thought the driver
   C would never get the car into it.
   D *(No mistakes)*

For number 6, find the underlined part that is the simple subject of the sentence.

6 Our <u>school's</u> <u>cafeteria</u> usually <u>serves</u> delicious <u>food</u>.
         F   G   H   J

For number 7, find the underlined part that is the simple predicate (verb) of the sentence.

7 A <u>set</u> of <u>shelves</u> <u>held</u> more than one <u>hundred</u> books.
     A   B   C   D

GO

For numbers 8-10, choose the answer that best combines the underlined sentences.

8   The squirrel ran up the tree.

    The squirrel ran quickly.

    F   The squirrel ran quickly up the tree.
    G   Up the tree quickly ran the squirrel.
    H   Quickly up the tree ran the squirrel.
    J   The squirrel ran up the tree, and ran quickly.

9   The smoke went up the chimney.

    The smoke is from the fireplace.

    A   The smoke, which went up the chimney, and was from the fireplace.
    B   From the fireplace went the smoke up the chimney.
    C   The smoke from the fireplace went up the chimney.
    D   Up the chimney went the smoke, which was from the fireplace.

10 Wanda is in line.

    The line is long.

    The line is for tickets to a new movie.

    F   The long line for tickets to a new movie is where Wanda is.
    G   Wanda is in a long line for tickets to a new movie.
    H   In a long line is Wanda for tickets to a new movie.
    J   The line for tickets to a new movie is long and Wanda is in it.

For numbers 11 and 12, choose the best way of expressing the idea.

11 A   No one was injured in a fire, and it damaged a factory near my home.
    B   A fire damaged a factory near my home, but no one was injured.
    C   Near my home, no one was injured, and a factory was damaged by a fire.
    D   A factory was damaged near my home by a fire which injured no one.

12 F   To raise money for library books, a snack shop was opened by our class last year.
    G   Our class opened a snack shop last year, and it was to raise money for library books.
    H   Last year, our class opened a snack shop to raise money for library books.
    J   A snack shop to raise money for library books was opened by our class last year.

GO

Read the paragraph below. Find the best topic sentence for the paragraph.

13 _____ . It is a large island, about the same size as Texas. Because of good weather and fertile soil, Madagascar has a strong farming economy. It is also the home of many unusual animal and plant species.

   A Madagascar, Australia, and New Zealand are all islands.

   B The first settlers in Madagascar were traders from Malaysia and Indonesia.

   C Madagascar is an island off the southeast coast of Africa.

   D An island's weather is affected by the body of water that surrounds it.

Find the answer choice that best develops the topic sentence.

14 The abacus is an ancient device for counting and making calculations.

   F It consists of a wooden frame and wires on which beads have been strung. By sliding the beads on the wires, a user can solve mathematics problems.

   G In some respects, an abacus is like a computer. Computers are used today to solve mathematics problems.

   H It was used most often in Asia. Many inventions, including printing and gunpowder, came from Asia to Europe.

   J Another mechanical calculating device is the slide rule. Because of hand-held calculators, you rarely see slide rules any more.

Read the paragraph below. Find the sentence that does not belong in the paragraph.

15 1. Archaeologists believe that Mexico was first settled more than 10,000 years ago.   2. These early settlers learned to grow plants such as corn, squash, and avocados.   3. They eventually developed many advanced civilizations and built wonderful cities.   4. Spanish is the language most Mexicans speak today.

   A Sentence 1

   B Sentence 2

   C Sentence 3

   D Sentence 4

Read the paragraph below. Find the sentence that best fits the blank in the paragraph.

16   Telecommunications is an exciting way to use a computer. _____. The modem allows computer signals to be sent over telephone lines. Many young people around the world are now using telecommunications to get to know one another.

   F A computer and a telephone are both electronic devices.

   G With a device called a modem, you can connect with other computers.

   H Computers can be found in many homes today.

   J Another exciting use of computers is called virtual reality.

GO >

Below is more of Giselle's report about gardening. Read her report and use it to do numbers 17-20.

Some unusual gardens have become popular today
(1)
One is the water garden. It is a small pond that
(2)   **(3)**
contains plants that grow best in or near water.

Fish, frogs, and turtles can be added to a water
(4)
garden to make it even more interesting.

The opposite of a water garden is a cactus
(5)
garden. There are many varieties of cactus that
(6)
have interesting shapes and beautiful flowers. In
(7)
cold climates, cactus plants can be brought in

during the winter. Spines protect cactus from
(8)
animals that might eat them.

A third type is the bonsai garden. Developed by
(9)   **(10)**
the Japanese, bonsai plants are miniature versions

of standard plants. A collection of bonsai plants
(11)
<u>make a wonderful</u> indoor garden.

17 How are sentences 2 and 3 best combined?

A The water garden, which is a small pond that contains plants that grow best in or near water.
B One is the water garden, a small pond that contains plants that grow best in or near water.
C A small pond, which is the water garden that contains plants that grow best in or near water.
D A small pond that contains plants, grow best in or near water, a water garden.

18 Which sentence does not belong in this report?

F 1
G 4
H 6
J 8

19 How is sentence 5 best written?

A The opposite, which is a cactus garden.
B The opposite of a water garden, a cactus garden.
C The opposite of a water garden that is a cactus garden.
D As it is

20 In sentence 11, <u>make a wonderful</u> is best written —

F making a wonderful
G make a wonderfuller
H makes a wonderful
J As it is

99

STOP

Part 3   Spelling

E1

The _____ popped off my coat.

A buton
B button
C buttin
D butun

E2

F <u>solid</u> rock

G small <u>increase</u>

H important <u>clyent</u>

J <u>weaken</u> a ceiling

For numbers 1-6, find the word that is spelled correctly and fits best in the blank.

1 The train came to an _____ stop.

A abrubt
B abrupt
C aprupt
D abrubd

2 Sheri _____ the leader in the race.

F ovrtook
G overtok
H overtoock
J overtook

3 His answer to the question was _____ .

A rapid
B rappd
C rappid
D wrapid

4 I think he is just talking _____ .

F nonsence
G nonsense
H nonsince
J nonsinse

5 Sending thank-you cards is a _____ I always follow.

A custim
B costum
C custom
D custem

6 An umbrella will _____ you from the sun.

F sheeld
G shield
H sheild
J shielt

For numbers 7-10, read the phrases. Choose the phrase in which the underlined word is **not** spelled correctly.

7 A less <u>crowded</u>

B very <u>gentle</u>

C <u>trade</u> pins

D <u>perfrom</u> well

8 F great <u>abilaty</u>

G <u>thought</u> hard

H can <u>achieve</u>

J <u>exact</u> change

9 A <u>lumber</u> yard

B wise <u>decision</u>

C clear <u>evadence</u>

D <u>string</u> popcorn

10 F <u>slanted</u> line

G <u>interpet</u> Spanish

H wonderful <u>celebration</u>

J <u>mistaken</u> idea

GO

For numbers 11-13, read each answer. Fill in the space for the choice that has a spelling error. If there is no mistake, fill in the last answer space.

11 A sketch
    B persist
    C exhibit
    D honesty
    E (No mistakes)

12 F resort
    G musical
    H apearance
    J disorder
    K (No mistakes)

13 A rainge
    B governor
    C person
    D guard
    E (No mistakes)

For numbers 14-16, read each phrase. One of the underlined words is not spelled correctly for the way it is used in the phrase. Fill in the space for the word that is not spelled correctly.

14 F spray water
    G exciting game
    H get organized
    J feel pried

15 A imitate him
    B soar arm
    C simple process
    D clear diagram

16 F good habit
    G earn income
    H least a car
    J select an item

For numbers 17-20, find the underlined part that is misspelled. If all the words are spelled correctly, mark the space under No mistake.

17 Be careful you don't sleid on the icy sidewalk. No mistake.
       A   B   C   D

18 The reasen the car stopped is because you ran out of gas. No mistake.
         F   G   H   J

19 The passengers of the airline were angry at the delay. No mistake.
          A   B   C   D

20 It took several days to reach the distent mountains. No mistake.
             F   G   H   J

STOP

```
            OUTLINE
Solar System
    1.  Sun
    2.  _____
    3.  Moons
    4.  Asteroids
    5.  Comets
```

E1

Which of these would fit best in Line 2 of the outline on the left?

A   Oceans
B   Planets
C   Rocket ships
D   Clouds

Study the newspaper below. Use it to do numbers 1-4.

| Monday | DAILY BUGLE | Today's Weather |
| June 6 | | Cloudy, high 78 |

INDEX
The Arts C1
Business & Money B7
Classified B4
Comics D5
Crossword D6
Local News A3
Opinion & Editorial A7
Sports B1
Teen Express C5
Weather A3
World News D1

Governor's Visit Delayed

Governor Alice King's press secretary announced this morning that the governor's trip to Centerville will be postponed for at least one month. "The governor is disappointed that she cannot visit her home town as scheduled, but she has been invited to Washington to meet with the President."

(Continued on page A4)

Fire Destroys Warehouse

A fire at 2:00 AM destroyed the warehouse of the Central Hardware Company. No one was injured in the blaze, and authorities are investigating to determine the cause.

(Photos on page A2)

The warehouse, located at 385 Industrial Street, was over 100 years old. The last person

(Continued on page A2)

1   How many sections does this paper have?

A   1
B   2
C   3
D   4

2   Which of these appears on page A2?

F   Opinion and Editorial
G   Sports
H   The continuation of the story about the warehouse fire
J   The continuation of the story about the governor

3   What was the weather on the day this newspaper was published?

A   Cloudy with a high temperature of 78°
B   Fair and sunny
C   It would be found on page D1.
D   It can't be determined.

4   In which section would you be most likely to find advertisements for used cars?

F   A
G   B
H   C
J   D

GO

Rich is writing a report about organic farming. Keep this purpose in mind when you do numbers 5-6.

5 Rich used the book titled *Profitable Organic Farming*. Where in the book should Rich look to find the definition of the term "intensive planting"?

    A the index
    B the table of contents
    C the glossary
    D the introduction

6 Which of these should Rich include in his report?

    F the names of the farmers in his state and where they live
    G a comparison of traditional and organic farming
    H the steps involved in building a barn to store organically grown crops
    J places where farmers can buy tractors and other equipment

For number 7, read the sentences. Then choose the key words Rich should include in his notes about organic farming.

7 Organic farming was long thought to be limited to home gardens. In recent years, however, many large-scale farms using organic methods have been successful and profitable. It is becoming clear that organic farming is good for the land and good for the pocketbook.

    A organic farming profitable and preserves land
    B used by home gardeners profitably
    C limited to home gardens but good for the land
    D large-scale farms in recent years

Study this dictionary entry. Then do numbers 8-10.

---

no·tice (nō′ tis) *Noun.* 1. information or warning about something *The weather service gave notice about the coming cold weather.* 2. a printed or written document giving information or a warning *A notice was posted about the election for mayor.* 3. a statement that an existing arrangement is to be ended *The employee gave the manager notice that she was retiring.* 4. attention or observation *Be sure to take notice of the plant life on the island.*
—*Verb.* 5. to observe *Did you notice how much Arthur has grown?*

---

8 Which definition of the word *notice* is used in this sentence?

A notice appeared in the paper informing parents about an open-house at the school.

    F Definition 2
    G Definition 3
    H Definition 4
    J Definition 5

9 Which definition of the word *notice* means to look at or see?

    A Definition 1
    B Definition 2
    C Definition 4
    D Definition 5

10 Which of these could be guide words on a dictionary page that includes the word *notice*?

    F notion/novice
    G nose/notary
    H nose/novice
    J normal/notary

STOP

Table of Contents
Math

Lesson 1   Numeration

Example   **Directions:** Read and work each problem. Find the correct answer.
Mark the space for your choice.

A Which group of numbers is ordered from greatest to least?

   A 1829, 1289, 9821, 2981

   B 1247, 1274, 4127, 7214

   C 6824, 8642, 6428, 4826

   D 5973, 5793, 5379, 3975

B Which of these is the expanded numeral for 7205?

   F 7000 + 200 + 50

   G 7000 + 200 + 5

   H 700 + 200 + 0 + 5

   J 7 + 2 + 0 + 5

Read the question carefully and look at all the answer choices before you mark the one you think is correct.

Be sure the answer circle you fill in is the same letter as the answer you think is correct.

Practice

1 $\sqrt{16}$

   A 7

   B 3

   C 8

   D 4

2 What is the greatest common factor of 18 and 54?

   F 18

   G 6

   H 9

   J 54

3 Which of these is a multiple of 11?

   A 101

   B 121

   C 111

   D 122

4 What number is expressed by
(9 x 10,000) + (4 x 1000) + (8 x 100) + (5 x 1)?

   F 9485

   G 94,085

   H 94,805

   J 910,485

5 Which of these is between 4,823,017 and 4,832,017?

   A 4,832,316

   B 4,892,316

   C 4,829,316

   D 4,823,016

6 Which of these is another way to write
8 x 8 x 8 x 8 x 8?

   F 5^8

   G 8^5

   H 8 x 5

   J 8 + 5

GO

7 Which numeral comes right after XI?

A   XII

B   IX

C   VI

D   XV

8 A worker in a warehouse has 68 bicycle tires to put into boxes. Each box can hold 12 tires. How many boxes will the worker need for all the tires?

F   5

G   6

H   12

J   10

9 Arnie wants to serve each of his friends a donut and a can of apple juice. There are 8 donuts in a pack, but only 6 cans of juice in a pack. What is the fewest number of donuts and cans of juice must Arnie buy so that he has the same number of each?

A   6

B   8

C   16

D   24

10 The expanded numeral for 52,070 is —

F $5 + 2 + 0 + 7 + 0$

G $(52 \times 10,000) + 70$

H $(5 \times 10,000) + (2 \times 1000) + (7 \times 10)$

J $(5 \times 1000) + (2 \times 100) + (7 \times 10)$

11 What are all the factors of 12?

A   2, 3, and 4

B   24, 36, and 48

C   2 and 6

D   1, 2, 3, 4, 6, and 12

12 What is the smallest number that can be divided evenly by 3 and 45?

F   125

G   15

H   90

J   120

13 $225 =$

A 25^2

B 12^2

C 2^5

D 15^2

14 What is the greatest common factor of 35 and 42?

F   7

G   9

H   3

J   5

15 Which of these is less than 124 and more than 110?

A   109

B   117

C   127

D   101

16 5 tens, 8 millions, 3 thousands, and 6 ones =

F   8,006,510

G   8,536,000

H   5836

J   8,003,056

STOP

Example   **Directions:** Read and work each problem. Find the correct answer. Mark the space for your choice.

A   Sixty-seven =
 	
    A 76
    B 67
    C 64
    D 77
	B The 5 in 35,902 means
	
	    F 50,000
	    G 5
	    H 500
	    J 5000

Look for key words and numbers that will help you find the answers. Remember, you might not have to compute to find the correct answer to a problem.

If a problem is too difficult, skip it and come back to it later.

Practice

1   What number is one thousand less than 509,183?

    A 409,183
    B 510,183
    C 508,183
    D 499,183

2   Which expression shows 50 as a multiple of prime numbers?

    F 2 x 5 x 5
    G 25 x 2
    H 5 x 10
    J 50 x 1

3   How many even numbers are there between 8 and 16?

    A 2
    B 5
    C 4
    D 3

4   A number is less than 539 and greater than 427. The sum of the ones digit and the tens digit in the number is 9. The ones digit is 4. What is the number?

    F 463
    G 454
    H 554
    J 418

5   What number is missing from the pattern shown below?

> 3, 8, 18, ___ , 78, 158

    A 28
    B 21
    C 38
    D 34

GO

6 Which of these numbers has a 7 in the tenths place?

F   2.0179

G   7.9201

H   9.7201

J   1.2709

7 Twenty thousand, nine =

A   29,000

B   20,100,009

C   20,090

D   20,009

8 Which of these is a prime number?

F   37

G   4

H   27

J   9

9 How much would the value of 284,079 be decreased by replacing the 8 with a 7?

A   1

B   10,000

C   100

D   1000

10 4,080,611 is read —

F   four hundred eight million, six hundred eleven

G   four million, eighty-six hundred eleven

H   four million, eighty thousand, six hundred eleven

J   forty-eight million, six hundred eleven

11 Which of these is a composite number?

A   18

B   13

C   29

D   41

12 Which numeral has a 3 in both the tens of thousands and ones places?

F   37,432

G   3903

H   23,913

J   31,043

13 What is the value of the 5 in 2.051?

A   5 tenths

B   5 hundredths

C   5 tens

D   5 thousandths

14 Which group contains both odd and even numbers?

F   46, 78, 92, 54, 36

G   19, 23, 57, 95, 31

H   21, 32, 47, 55, 68

J   22, 36, 44, 68, 90

15 A number has a 9 in the tens place, a 3 in the ones place, and a 4 in the thousands place. Which number is it?

A   493

B   4793

C   7493

D   349

STOP

Example   **Directions:** Read and work each problem. Find the correct answer. Mark the space for your choice.

A Which is another name for 320 x 1000?

   A 32 x 100

   B 3200 x 100

   C 321 x 1000

   D 3 x 2100

B What is 237 rounded to the nearest hundred?

   F 200

   G 300

   H 100

   J 230

Take the best guess when you are unsure of the answer.

When you work on scratch paper, be sure to transfer numbers accurately and compute carefully.

Practice

1 $\frac{4}{\square} = \frac{24}{42}$

   $\square =$

   A 7

   B 20

   C 14

   D 6

2 Which is another name for 45?

   F (4 x 5) + 10

   G 4 + (5 x 1)

   H 51 – (3 x 2)

   J (3 x 3) x 6

3 The product of 497 x 21.89 is closest to —

   A 100

   B 10,000

   C 800

   D 8000

4 What number goes in the box to make this sentence true?

   $\square > -9$

   F –15

   G –9

   H –12

   J –1

5 Which of these statements is true?

   A When a whole number is multiplied by 3, the product will always be an odd number.

   B When a whole number is multiplied by 2, the product will always be an even number.

   C All numbers that can be divided by 5 are odd numbers.

   D The product of an even and odd number is always an odd number.

GO

6 Which number completes the number sentence below?

$$4 \times (3 + 5) = \square + 17$$

F 11

G 6

H 0

J 15

7 There are 52 weeks in a year. Willard works for 48 weeks, and during each week, he works 40 hours. Which number sentence below shows how many hours Willard works in a year?

A $52 \times 40 = \square$

B $48 \times 40 = \square$

C $48 \times 52 = \square$

D $(52 - 48) \times 40 = \square$

8 Which of the tables below follows the rule shown below?

Rule: Add 4 to the number in column A, then multiply by 6 to get the number in column B.

A	B
2	36
3	42
5	54
7	66

F

A	B
2	16
3	22
5	34
7	46

G

A	B
2	12
3	16
5	15
7	17

H

A	B
2	48
3	72
5	120
7	168

J

9 A number rounded to the nearest hundred is 23,200. The same number rounded to the nearest thousand is 23,000. Which of these could be the number?

A 22,914

B 23,681

C 23,168

D 23, 099

10 In which of the situations below would you probably use an estimate?

F You owe a friend some money and you want to pay the friend back.

G You are the manager and are calculating the batting averages for the players on your school baseball team.

H You are responsible for counting the votes in the school election.

J You want to tell some friends how many bees are in a hive.

11 For your science project, you planted 50 flower seeds. You found that 20 of the seeds didn't grow at all, and $\frac{2}{3}$ of the rest had red flowers. Which of the number sentences below show how to find the number of plants that had red flowers?

A $50 - 20 = \frac{2}{3} \times \square$

B $\frac{2}{3} \times (50 - 20) = \square$

C $(\frac{2}{3} \times 50) - 20 = \square$

D $(\frac{2}{3} \times 20) = \square$

STOP

Example   **Directions:** Read and work each problem. Find the correct answer. Mark the space for your choice.

A How much of the figure on the right is shaded?

A $\frac{1}{2}$

B $\frac{3}{5}$

C $\frac{5}{8}$

D $\frac{1}{5}$

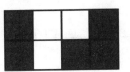

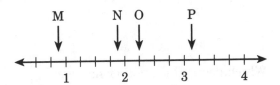

Pay close attention to the numbers in the problem and in the answer choices. If you misread even one number, you will probably choose the wrong answer.

Eliminate answer choices you know are wrong.

Practice

1 Which of these is four hundredths?

A 0.400

B 0.004

C 4.100

D 0.040

2 $\frac{72}{1000} =$

F 7.200

G 0.7200

H 0.072

J 0.72

3 Which of these is greater than $\frac{3}{4}$?

A $\frac{1}{2}$

B $\frac{2}{9}$

C $\frac{3}{5}$

D $\frac{7}{8}$

4 On the number line below, which arrow points most closely to 1.9?

F M

G N

H O

J P

5 Which of these is between 0.08 and 0.4 in value?

A 0.19

B 0.91

C 0.009

D 0.019

GO ⟩

6 The length of $\overline{ST}$ is what fraction of the length of $\overline{OP}$?

O └┴┴┴┴┴┴┴┴┴┴┘ P

S └┴┴┴┴┴┴┘ T

F $\frac{1}{6}$

G $\frac{3}{4}$

H $\frac{7}{10}$

J $\frac{3}{5}$

7 What is the least common denominator for $\frac{1}{2}$, $\frac{4}{5}$, and $\frac{2}{3}$?

A 60

B 15

C 30

D 10

8 Which decimal is another name for $\frac{2}{1000}$?

F 0.002

G 0.2000

H 2

J 0.0200

9 Which group of decimals is ordered from least to greatest?

A 4.081   1.804   1.048   1.408

B 1.048   1.408   1.804   4.081

C 0.481   1.408   4.801   0.841

D 0.841   0.481   8.401   8.014

10 Which of these numbers can go in the box to make this number sentence true?

$$\frac{1}{\square} > \frac{1}{3}$$

F 2

G 3

H 6

J 5

11 Which fraction is another name for $4\frac{2}{5}$?

A $\frac{8}{5}$

B $\frac{20}{2}$

C $\frac{42}{5}$

D $\frac{22}{5}$

12 Which fraction is in simplest form?

F $\frac{4}{8}$

G $\frac{6}{11}$

H $\frac{5}{15}$

J $\frac{2}{12}$

13 Which of the decimals below is twenty-five and seventeen hundredths?

A 2517

B 25.17

C 25.017

D 2500.17

112

STOP

Examples   Directions: Read each question. Find the correct answer. Mark the space for your choice.

E1

Which of these groups of numbers is in order from greatest to least?

A 18,492 14,289 14,928 12,498

B 12,498 14,928 14,982 18,492

C 18,492 14,982 14,928 12,498

D 14,982 12,498 18,492 14,928

E2

What is 1847 rounded to the nearest hundred?

F 1800

G 1900

H 1850

J 1840

---

1 Which digit means ten thousands in the numeral 4,920,376?

A 2

B 0

C 3

D 9

2 Which of these numbers best shows what part of the bar is shaded?

F $\frac{1}{2}$

G 0.8

H 0.6

J $\frac{2}{3}$

3 Which letter marks $6\frac{3}{10}$ on this number line?

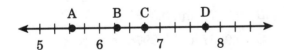

A A

B B

C C

D D

4 6132 ÷ 19 is between —

F 100 and 200

G 400 and 500

H 150 and 250

J 250 and 350

5 Which of these is a composite number?

A 17

B 61

C 16

D 43

6 In a book, which chapter comes right before Chapter IX?

F Chapter V

G Chapter XI

H Chapter X

J Chapter VIII

7 Which of these is another way to write 508,062?

A 50 + 80 + 60 + 2

B 50,000 + 8000 + 60 + 2

C 500,000 + 8000 + 60 + 2

D 500,000 + 80,000 + 60 + 2

GO ▷

---

8 What number is missing from the pattern below?

$$\frac{1}{5}, 0.3, \frac{4}{10}, 0.5, \underline{\quad}, 0.7$$

F $\frac{5}{10}$

G 6.0

H $\frac{6}{10}$

J 0.06

9 Suppose you had 30 rolls and wanted to put them into bags that could hold 8 rolls each. How many bags could you fill completely?

A 4

B 3

C 6

D 8

10 Which of these symbols goes in the circle to make this number sentence true?

$$\frac{9}{10} + \frac{3}{4} \bigcirc 2$$

F ≥

G =

H >

J <

11 What is 0.583 rounded to the nearest tenth?

A 0.6

B 0.5

C 0.06

D 0.1

12 $\sqrt{100} =$

F 10

G 1000

H 11

J 25

13 Which is the numeral for seven hundred nine thousand, two hundred thirty nine?

A 7,009,000,239

B 79,239

C 709,239

D 792,039

14 What number completes this number sentence?

$$3 \times 29 = 3 \times (\square + 9)$$

F 26

G 32

H 2

J 20

15 Using the digits 3, 7, 8, and 9, which of the following are the largest and smallest decimal numbers you can write?

A 0.8973 and 0.7398

B 0.9873 and 0.3789

C 0.9837 and 0.3978

D 0.9783 and 0.3879

STOP

ANSWER ROWS
114
8 F G H J   11 A B C D   14 F G H J
9 A B C D   12 F G H J   15 A B C D
10 F G H J   13 A B C D

NUMBER RIGHT_____

Lesson 6   Addition

Example   **Directions:** Mark the space for the correct answer to each addition problem. Choose "None of these" if the right answer is not given.

A		A 51
		B 46
48		C 68
+ 2		D 50
		E None of these

B		F 24
		G 2.04
2 + 0.4 = ☐		H 20.4
		J 0.6
		K None of these

If the answer you find is not one of the answer choices, rework the problem on scratch paper.

If you rework a problem and still find that the right answer is not given, mark the space for "None of these."

Practice

1
20.8
+ 4.1

  A 204.9
  B 249
  C   24.9
  D   24.81
  E None of these

5
587
623
+ 205

  A 1405
  B 1415
  C 1715
  D   515
  E None of these

2
6852
+ 3074

  F 9826
  G 3822
  H 3798
  J 9962
  K None of these

6
$5.10
+ 0.95

  F $5.95
  G $6.05
  H $50.95
  J $51.05
  K None of these

3
$\frac{1}{9} + \frac{1}{9} = \square$

  A $\frac{2}{9}$
  B $\frac{1}{18}$
  C $\frac{2}{18}$
  D $\frac{1}{10}$
  E None of these

7
$29 + \square = 100$

  A 129
  B   61
  C 291
  D   71
  E None of these

4
$0.367 + 0.821 =$

  F 1.088
  G 0.1188
  H 1.188
  J 1.118
  K None of these

8
$\frac{1}{13} + \frac{6}{13} =$

  F 5
  G $\frac{7}{13}$
  H $\frac{5}{13}$
  J $\frac{1}{2}$
  K None of these

GO

9

$3\frac{1}{7}$

$+\ 6\frac{1}{7}$

  A $9\frac{2}{14}$

  B   10

  C   3

  D $9\frac{2}{7}$

  E   None of these

14

$\$4.33 + \$8.09 =$

  F $12.42

  G $13.23

  H $12.39

  J $4.24

  K   None of these

10

6722
246
73
$+\ 158$

  F   7199

  G   6999

  H   7189

  J   6199

  K   None of these

15

$\frac{7}{10}$

$+\ \frac{9}{10}$

  A $\frac{1}{5}$

  B $\frac{16}{20}$

  C $1\frac{3}{5}$

  D $1\frac{1}{6}$

  E   None of these

11

$\frac{4}{11} + \frac{6}{11} =$

  A $\frac{2}{11}$

  B   1

  C $\frac{10}{11}$

  D $\frac{2}{5}$

  E   None of these

16

$3200 + 5138 + 864 =$

  F   8204

  G   9192

  H   8212

  J   9202

  K   None of these

12

235.26
$+\ \ \ 61.41$

  F   234.25

  G   296.67

  H   266.67

  J   294.67

  K   None of these

17

$\frac{3}{5} + \frac{7}{10} = \square$

  A $1\frac{3}{5}$

  B $\frac{10}{15}$

  C $\frac{2}{3}$

  D   1

  E   None of these

13

$\frac{1}{9}$

$+\ \frac{1}{18}$

  A $\frac{1}{27}$

  B $\frac{1}{9}$

  C $\frac{2}{27}$

  D $\frac{1}{3}$

  E   None of these

18

$\$65.14 + \$27.93 =$

  F $103.07

  G $92.07

  H $93.07

  J $92.87

  K   None of these

STOP

Example   **Directions:** Mark the space for the correct answer to each subtraction problem. Choose "NG" if the right answer is not given.

A		
33 – 5 = ☐	**A** 28	
	B 38	
	C 27	
	D 18	
	E NG	

B		
424 – 39	**F** 0.29	
	G 1.1	
	H 384	
	J 395	
	K NG	

If the right answer is not given, mark the space for "NG." This means "not given."

When you are not sure of an answer, check it by adding.

Practice

1

633
– 47

   A 614
   B 594
   C 616
   D 686
   E NG

5

7.86
– 1.87

   A 6.01
   B 6.09
   C 5.19
   D 5.99
   E NG

2

0.914 – 0.286 =

   F 1.2
   G 0.772
   H 0.782
   J 0.628
   K NG

6

0.406 – 0.007 =

   F 0.301
   G 0.491
   H 0.391
   J 0.401
   K NG

3

8005 – 2274 = ☐

   A 10,279
   B 5731
   C 6871
   D 5871
   E NG

7

41 – 27 =

   A 4
   B 24
   C 14
   D 26
   E NG

4

29,111
– 725

   F 29,836
   G 29,614
   H 28,614
   J 28,386
   K NG

8

534
– 249

   F 285
   G 315
   H 385
   J 305
   K NG

GO ▷

9

$7\frac{5}{10}$
$- 3\frac{1}{2}$

A $4\frac{4}{10}$
B 11
C $4\frac{4}{8}$
D 4
E NG

10

$\frac{12}{15} - \frac{2}{5} =$

F $\frac{1}{5}$
G 0
H $\frac{2}{3}$
J 1
K NG

11

$\frac{5}{6}$
$- \frac{4}{6}$

A $\frac{1}{6}$
B $\frac{1}{12}$
C 1
D 0
E NG

12

$1 - \frac{1}{7} =$

F $\frac{1}{6}$
G $\frac{7}{6}$
H $\frac{6}{7}$
J $\frac{2}{7}$
K NG

13

$50.00 - $32.06 =

A $27.94
B $18.06
C $18.94
D $17.94
E NG

14

82,346
− 7,867

F 85,521
G 90,213
H 74,479
J 84,479
K NG

15

15.227
− 14.043

A 1.184
B 29.27
C 1.224
D 0.184
E NG

16

5.5 − 0.28 =

F 5.528
G 5.22
H 5.28
J 5.78
K NG

17

3000 − 243 =

A 3243
B 3867
C 3757
D 2747
E NG

18

879
− 94

F 875
G 825
H 785
J 725
K NG

19 Estimate the answer for this item.

54,729 − 1928
is closest to

A 57,000
B 55,000
C 51,000
D 53,000
E NG

STOP

Example

Directions: Mark the space for the correct answer to each multiplication problem. Choose "NH" if the right answer is not given.

A			B	
41 x 4	**A** 45 **B** 164 **C** 85 **D** 441 **E** NH		0.5 x 12 =	**F** 5.2 **G** 60 **H** 11.5 **J** 8 **K** NH

If the right answer is not given, mark the space for "NH." This means "not here."

When you multiply large numbers, be sure to align the numbers correctly. In decimal problems, remember to insert the decimal point in the right place.

Practice

1

$\begin{array}{r} 4 \\ \times 7 \\ \hline \end{array}$

A 11
B 24
C 28
D 3
E NH

2

4 x 5000 =

F 2000
G 45,000
H 20,000
J 9000
K NH

3

$\begin{array}{r} 24 \\ \times 86 \\ \hline \end{array}$

A 2064
B 2846
C 11,344
D 19,344
E NH

4

0.9 x 0.2 =

F 0.018
G 1.8
H 0.29
J 18
K NH

5

$8 \times \frac{1}{9} =$

A $1\frac{1}{8}$
B $\frac{8}{9}$
C $1\frac{1}{9}$
D $\frac{1}{72}$
E NH

6

$\begin{array}{r} 810 \\ \times 62 \\ \hline \end{array}$

F 5220
G 50,222
H 50,220
J 49,220
K NH

7

☐ x 50 = 1250

A 210
B 25
C 120
D 75
E NH

8

$\begin{array}{r} 9.18 \\ \times 3.7 \\ \hline \end{array}$

F 39.187
G 39.178
H 27.178
J 33.966
K NH

GO

9

$\frac{2}{3} \times 12 =$

A 9
B $8\frac{3}{4}$
C $\frac{1}{18}$
D 8
E NG

10

$\frac{3}{5} \times \frac{1}{9} =$

F $3\frac{1}{45}$
G 4
H $\frac{3}{44}$
J $\frac{4}{45}$
K NG

11

$\frac{1}{5}$
$\times 4$

A $4\frac{1}{20}$
B $5\frac{1}{20}$
C $\frac{4}{5}$
D $20\frac{1}{5}$
E NG

12

$\frac{2}{3} \times \frac{5}{8} =$

F $\frac{5}{12}$
G $1\frac{5}{8}$
H $7\frac{1}{24}$
J $\frac{7}{11}$
K NG

13

$0.07 \times 20 = \square$

A 140
B 1.4
C 20.7
D 0.27
E NG

14

$.4 \times .9 =$

F 0.32
G 0.036
H 3.6
J 36
K NG

15

370
$\times \ 31$

A 11,470
B 401
C 1480
D 14,170
E NG

16

$3 \times 12 = \square$

F 15
G 45
H 35
J 36
K NG

17

$4 \times 826 =$

A 3300
B 3304
C 3324
D 3704
E NG

18

1479
$\times \ 304$

F 349,616
G 449,612
H 449,616
J 349,612
K NG

19 Estimate the answer for this item.

103×11
is closest to

A 1000
B 100
C 10,000
D 11,000
E NG

STOP

ANSWER ROWS   **9** Ⓐ Ⓑ Ⓒ Ⓓ Ⓔ   **12** Ⓕ Ⓖ Ⓗ Ⓙ Ⓚ   **15** Ⓐ Ⓑ Ⓒ Ⓓ Ⓔ   **18** Ⓕ Ⓖ Ⓗ Ⓙ Ⓚ
120   **10** Ⓕ Ⓖ Ⓗ Ⓙ Ⓚ   **13** Ⓐ Ⓑ Ⓒ Ⓓ Ⓔ   **16** Ⓕ Ⓖ Ⓗ Ⓙ Ⓚ   **19** Ⓐ Ⓑ Ⓒ Ⓓ Ⓔ
   11 Ⓐ Ⓑ Ⓒ Ⓓ Ⓔ   **14** Ⓕ Ⓖ Ⓗ Ⓙ Ⓚ   **17** Ⓐ Ⓑ Ⓒ Ⓓ Ⓔ

Example   **Directions:** Mark the space for the correct answer to each division problem. Choose "N" if the right answer is not given.

A		A 7	B		F 14
$7\overline{)50}$		B 8 C 17 D N	$8.4 \div 7 =$		G 12 H 1.2 J N

Pay close attention when you are dividing decimals or fractions. It is easy to make a mistake by misplacing the decimal point or forgetting to invert fractions.

If the right answer is not given, mark the space for "N." This means the answer is not given.

Practice

1

$44 \div 4 =$

A 40
B 10
C 21
D N

5

$29\overline{)2378}$

A 82
B 81 R3
C 82 R8
D N

2

$6\overline{)86}$

F 16
G 14 R2
H 12 R4
J N

6

$67 \div 15 =$

F 5 R2
G 5
H 4
J N

3

$\frac{1}{7} \div 7 =$

A 1
B $\frac{1}{7}$
C $\frac{1}{49}$
D N

7

$2\overline{)6.8}$

A 34
B 3.2
C 3.4
D N

4

$7\overline{)105}$

F 15
G 12 R5
H 13
J N

8

$96 \div 12 = \square$

F 92
G 8
H 4
J N

GO

9

$280 \div 20 =$

A 300
B 12
C 14
D N

10

$4\overline{)59}$

F 15
G 14 R3
H 16 R3
J N

11

$7.56 \div 3.6 =$

A 2.1
B 21
C 3.96
D N

12

$32 \div 8 = \square$

F 3 R4
G 4 R1
H 5
J N

13

$6\overline{)385}$

A 215
B $64\frac{1}{6}$
C $65\frac{5}{6}$
D N

14

$\frac{7}{8} \div \frac{1}{4} =$

F $3\frac{1}{2}$
G $1\frac{3}{4}$
H $\frac{7}{32}$
J N

15

$26\overline{)442}$

A 17
B 16 R2
C 22
D N

16

$27,000 \div 300 =$

F 900
G 90
H 70
J N

17

$29\overline{)2378}$

A 78
B 182
C 72
D N

18

$20.4 \div 5$

F 15.4
G 4.1
H 4.08
J N

19

$63\overline{)5106}$

A 81 R3
B 86
C 80 R6
D N

20 Estimate the answer for this item.

$3794 \div 19$
is closest to

F 20
G 300
H 200
J N

STOP

ANSWER ROWS
122

9 Ⓐ Ⓑ Ⓒ Ⓓ   12 Ⓕ Ⓖ Ⓗ Ⓙ   15 Ⓐ Ⓑ Ⓒ Ⓓ   18 Ⓕ Ⓖ Ⓗ Ⓙ
10 Ⓕ Ⓖ Ⓗ Ⓙ   13 Ⓐ Ⓑ Ⓒ Ⓓ   16 Ⓕ Ⓖ Ⓗ Ⓙ   19 Ⓐ Ⓑ Ⓒ Ⓓ
11 Ⓐ Ⓑ Ⓒ Ⓓ   14 Ⓕ Ⓖ Ⓗ Ⓙ   17 Ⓐ Ⓑ Ⓒ Ⓓ   20 Ⓕ Ⓖ Ⓗ Ⓙ

Examples   Directions: Read and work each problem. Find the correct answer. Mark the space for your choice.

E1		E2	
940 − 61	A 1001 B 821 C 921 D 879 E None of these	411 x 9 =	F 4911 G 9411 H 420 J 3966 K None of these

1   6.44 ÷ 46 =

A 40.44
B 39.56
C 0.14
D 7.14
E None of these

6 $65.14 + $27.93 =

F $93.07
G $103.07
H $93.87
J $103.87
K None of these

2
387
691
+ 433

F 1510
G 1411
H 1521
J 1421
K None of these

7   40)3600

A 8
B 80
C 90
D 900
E None of these

3
293
x 11

A 304
B 3223
C 282
D 2223
E None of these

8
14
x 4

F 10
G 416
H 18
J 56
K None of these

4   71 − 28 =

F 99
G 53
H 43
J 57
K None of these

9
8.78
− .26

A 2.2828
B 6.18
C 8.16
D 8.52
E None of these

5 $5\frac{3}{8} - 2\frac{5}{8} =$

A $3\frac{1}{9}$
B $2\frac{3}{4}$
C $2\frac{1}{9}$
D $3\frac{1}{9}$
E None of these

10 $[(6 \times 4) + (2 \times 9)] \div 7 =$

F 7
G 35
H 6
J 46
K None of these

GO

ANSWER ROWS   E1 Ⓐ Ⓑ Ⓒ Ⓓ Ⓔ   2 Ⓕ Ⓖ Ⓗ Ⓙ Ⓚ   5 Ⓐ Ⓑ Ⓒ Ⓓ Ⓔ   8 Ⓕ Ⓖ Ⓗ Ⓙ Ⓚ
E2 Ⓕ Ⓖ Ⓗ Ⓙ Ⓚ   3 Ⓐ Ⓑ Ⓒ Ⓓ Ⓔ   6 Ⓕ Ⓖ Ⓗ Ⓙ Ⓚ   9 Ⓐ Ⓑ Ⓒ Ⓓ Ⓔ
1 Ⓐ Ⓑ Ⓒ Ⓓ Ⓔ   4 Ⓕ Ⓖ Ⓗ Ⓙ Ⓚ   7 Ⓐ Ⓑ Ⓒ Ⓓ Ⓔ   10 Ⓕ Ⓖ Ⓗ Ⓙ Ⓚ

123

11

$9\frac{4}{9} + \frac{5}{9} =$

A 10
B $9\frac{1}{9}$
C $10\frac{1}{9}$
D $9\frac{8}{9}$
E None of these

12

$0.4 \times 61.7 =$

F 246.8
G 24.68
H 614.7
J 268
K None of these

13

$\begin{array}{r} 4063 \\ -\ 507 \end{array}$

A 3564
B 4570
C 3464
D 3556
E None of these

14

$800\overline{)9432}$

F 12
G 11 R232
H 11 R32
J 11
K None of these

15

$5.58 - 2.99 =$

A 3.41
B 2.69
C 2.59
D 2.99
E None of these

16

$427 \div 7 =$

F 420
G 60 R6
H 434
J 61
K None of these

17

$\begin{array}{r} 211 \\ 14 \\ 43 \\ +\ 46 \end{array}$

A 414
B 2105
C 314
D 204
E None of these

18

$20.33 - .76 =$

F 19.57
G 21.09
H 20.57
J 19.43
K None of these

19

$\begin{array}{r} 83 \\ \times\ 43 \end{array}$

A 3209
B 3569
C 3669
D 4833
E None of these

20

$1780 \div 86 =$

F 21
G 20 R80
H 26
J 20 R40
K None of these

21

$\begin{array}{r} 7\frac{1}{4} \\ -\ 1\frac{7}{8} \end{array}$

A $6\frac{3}{4}$
B $5\frac{3}{8}$
C 6
D $6\frac{3}{8}$
E None of these

22

$8 \times \frac{3}{8} =$

F 24
G 3
H 38
J 4
K None of these

STOP

Lesson 11   Geometry

Example   **Directions:** Find the correct answer to each geometry problem. Mark the space for your choice.

A What is the perimeter of the figure on the right?

A 38 ft

B 52 ft

C 46 ft

D 168 ft

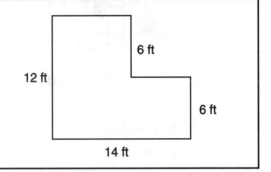

Read the question carefully and think about what you are supposed to do. Then look for key words, numbers, and figures before you choose an answer.

Practice

---

1 Which figure shows a point and three rays?

A

B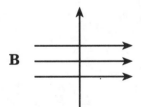

C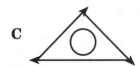

D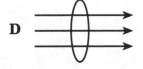

2 Two lines in the same plane that intersect at a right angle are —

F parallel

G curved

H perpendicular

J similar

3 What is the area of a room that is 15 meters long and 6 meters wide?

A 80 square meters

B 42 square meters

C 21 square meters

D 90 square meters

4 The measure of the amount of liquid a glass can hold is its —

F outside surface area

G volume

H inside surface area

J circumference

GO

---

5   What is the area of the shaded shape?

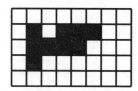

☐ = 1 square unit

A   8 square units

B   12 square units

C   6 square units

D   9 square units

6   How many faces does the figure below have?

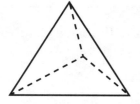

F   6

G   4

H   9

J   3

7   Which of the figures below are congruent?

A   2 and 3

B   2 and 1

C   1 and 4

D   4 and 3

8   Each block on the figure below is one cubic unit. How many cubic units are in the volume of the figure?

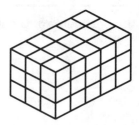

F   45

G   39

H   29

J   36

9   Which of the angles below is acute?

A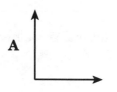

B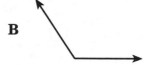

C

D

10 When two faces of a cube come together is called —

F   a vertex

G   an edge

H   a point

J   a ray

GO

11 Which of these is not a cone?

A   B

C   D

12 Which of these angles seems to be 90°?

F

G

H

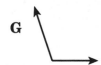

J

13 Which line segment is 9 units long?

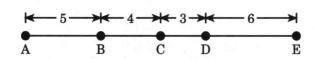

A $\overline{BD}$

B $\overline{AD}$

C $\overline{CE}$

D $\overline{BE}$

14 A storage room is 4 meters wide, 5 meters long, and 3 meters high. What is the volume of the room?

F 11 cubic meters

G 23 cubic meters

H 80 cubic meters

J 60 cubic meters

15 Which of these would you use to draw a circle?

A protractor

B compass

C thermometer

D ruler

16 A plane figure with 6 sides is called —

F an octagon

G an apex

H a pentagon

J a hexagon

17 Which pair of shapes below form mirror images?

A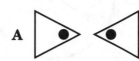

B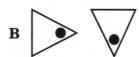

C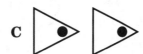

D

STOP

ANSWER ROWS **11** Ⓐ Ⓑ Ⓒ Ⓓ   **13** Ⓐ Ⓑ Ⓒ Ⓓ   **15** Ⓐ Ⓑ Ⓒ Ⓓ   **17** Ⓐ Ⓑ Ⓒ Ⓓ

12 Ⓕ Ⓖ Ⓗ Ⓙ   **14** Ⓕ Ⓖ Ⓗ Ⓙ   **16** Ⓕ Ⓖ Ⓗ Ⓙ

Example   **Directions:** Find the correct answer to each measurement problem. Mark the space for your choice.

A About how many centimeters long is the rectangle on the right?

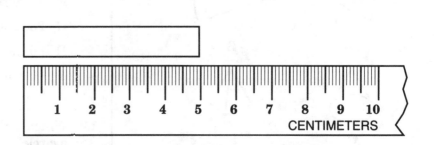

A 4 centimeters

B 5 centimeters

C 6 centimeters

D 10 centimeters

Before you choose an answer, ask yourself, "Does this answer make sense?"

If you are confused by a problem, read it again. If you are still confused, skip the problem and come back to it later.

Practice

1 A train leaves Chicago at 9 P.M. and reaches Denver 14 hours later. Which clock shows what time the train will arrive in Denver?

A

B

C

D

2 A hamburger weighs —

F a few ounces

G a few pounds

H a few grams

J a few milligrams

3 How many milliliters are equal to 2.81 liters? (1 liter = 1000 milliliters)

A 28.10 milliliters

B 2810.0 milliliters

C 2000.81 milliliters

D 0.00281 milliliters

4 Gary has 10 quarters, 6 half-dollars, 4 nickels, 14 dimes, and 37 pennies. How much money does he have in all?

F $6.87

G $7.37

H $7.47

J $6.97

GO

5 The scale on a map shows that 1 inch equals 8 miles. About how long would a section of road be that is 2.5 inches on the map?

A 25 miles

B 10.5 miles

C 16 miles

D 20 miles

6 What fraction of a pound is 2 ounces?

F $\frac{1}{8}$

G $\frac{1}{2}$

H $\frac{1}{4}$

J $\frac{1}{9}$

7 What temperature will the thermometer show if the temperature rises 14°.

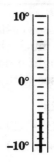

A −15°

B −19°

C 9°

D 19°

8 Margo's bed is about 2 yards long. About how many inches long is her bed?

F 24 inches

G 72 inches

H 6 inches

J 36 inches

9 About how many centimeters long is this picture of a safety pin?

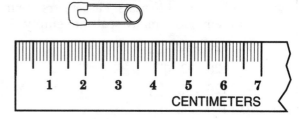

A 2 cm

B 3 cm

C 4 cm

D 7 cm

10 What is the ratio of two days to four weeks?

F $\frac{1}{2}$

G $\frac{1}{14}$

H $\frac{1}{7}$

J $\frac{1}{16}$

11 A basketball game started at 7:15 P.M. and lasted 2 hours and 50 minutes. What time did the game end?

A 9:50 P.M.

B 9:55 P.M.

C 10:55 P.M.

D 10:05 P.M.

12 Cindy is building a dog house. It will be 32 inches high. Another way to describe the height of the dog house is to say it is —

F a little more than 1 yard high

G a little less than 2 feet high

H a little less than 1 yard high

J a little more than 4 feet high

STOP

Lesson 13　Problem Solving

Example

Directions: Find the correct answer to each problem. Mark the space for your choice.

A A plane has 120 seats. Passengers are in 92 of them. How many seats are empty? **A** 120 ÷ 92 = ☐ **B** 120 - 92 = ☐ **C** 120 x 92 = ☐ **D** 120 + 92 = ☐	**B** If you mix 12 ounces of flour and 6 ounces of sugar, how much will it weigh all together? **F** 19 ounces **G** 6 ounces **H** 72 ounces **J** Not Given

Choose "Not Given" only if you are sure the right answer is not one of the choices.

Look for key words, numbers, and figures in each problem, and be sure you perform the correct operation.

Practice

1 A store is open for 12 hours a day. Each hour, an average of 15 customers comes into the store. How many customers come into the store in a day?

    A 15 x 24 = ☐
    B 12 + 15 = ☐
    C 12 x 15 = ☐
    D 24 ÷ 12 = ☐

3 A pair of sun glasses costs $12.95 and a hat costs $7.25. How much change would you receive if you bought a pair of glasses and paid for the glasses with a $20 bill?

    A $20 - ☐ = $7.25
    B ($12.95 + $7.25) - $20 = ☐
    C $20 - ($12.95 + $7.25) = ☐
    D $20 - $12.95 = ☐

2 Margarita is helping her father build a deck. The surface of the deck will be 10 feet wide and 14 feet long. The boards they are using for the deck can cover an area of 4 square feet. Which of these shows how many boards they will they need to cover the surface of the deck?

    F (10 x 14) ÷ 4 = ☐
    G (10 x 14) x 4 = ☐
    H 10 + 14 + 4 = ☐
    J (10 ÷ 14) x 4 = ☐

4 Dave, Kate, and Marcia went fishing. The fish they caught weighed $4\frac{1}{4}$, $6\frac{1}{2}$, and $2\frac{3}{4}$ pounds. How many pounds of fish did they catch in all?

    F $12\frac{3}{4}$
    G $13\frac{1}{2}$
    H $14\frac{1}{4}$
    J $13\frac{1}{4}$

GO

The graph below shows the scores earned by four students on two different tests. Use the graph to answer questions 5, 6, and 7.

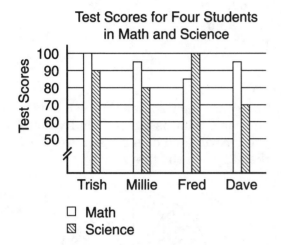

Test Scores for Four Students in Math and Science

☐ Math
▨ Science

5 What was Fred's score on the math test?

A 85
B 100
C 95
D 80

6 Who had the lowest score on the science test?

F Trish
G Dave
H Millie
J Not Given

7 What is the average score on the science test?

A 80
B 92
C 78
D 85

8 The supermarket in the town of Garret has 18 full-time workers and 7 part-time workers. How many more full-time workers are there than part-time workers?

F 25
G 19
H 12
J 11

9 Diane has been hired by the supermarket as a part-time worker. She will earn $5.50 an hour, and she hopes to work 12 hours each week. How much will she earn in a week?

A $66.00
B $56.50
C $17.50
D $60.50

10 If Diane stays on the job for 6 months, she will receive a $.50 an hour raise. If she stays 6 more months, she will receive another raise of $.75. How much will Diane earn if she stays on the job for 12 more months?

F $1.25
G $6.00
H $6.75
J Not Given

11 A can of soup at the market costs $.69, a loaf of bread costs $1.19, and a bunch of bananas is $1.25. During a sale, the price of each of the items was reduced by $.10. How much would it cost to buy all three items during the sale?

A $3.13
B $3.03
C $2.38
D Not Given

GO

The chart below shows the percentage of time different radio stations devote to music, talk, and advertisements. Some of the stations are east of the Mississippi River and others are west of the river. Use the chart to answer questions 12 through 14.

		MUSIC	TALK	ADS
EAST	WXYZ	11%	60%	29%
	WNMV	—	78%	22%
	WAAX	46%	27%	27%
WEST	KZAV	62%	20%	18%
	KQRT	75%	—	25%
	KBXC	25%	50%	25%

12 Which radio station has the highest percentage of time spent on talk?

F KZAV

G WXYZ

H WNMV

J KBXC

13 What percentage of the time does WAAX spend on music and ads all together?

A 63%

B 54%

C 64%

D Not Given

14 Which of these statements about the chart is true?

F Stations that are east of the Mississippi usually devote more time to ads.

G Stations that are west of the Mississippi usually devote more time to talk.

H Two stations devote none of their time to music.

J The station with the lowest percentage of time devoted to ads has the highest percentage of music.

15 It takes 4 workers about 18 hours to build a garage. How long would it take to build a garage if there were 12 workers?

A 54 hours

B 6 hours

C 3 hours

D Not Given

16 The game-show spinner below has 12 equal divisions. What is the probability that the pointer will land on a division worth more than $200 on the first spin?

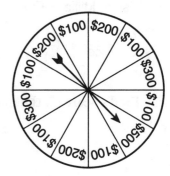

F $\frac{1}{12}$

G $\frac{1}{9}$

H $\frac{1}{4}$

J Not Given

17 A group of office workers are ordering sandwiches from the deli. They can choose ham, beef, turkey, or chicken on whole wheat bread, rye bread, or white bread. How many different meat and bread combinations are possible?

A 12

B 7

C 16

D Not Given

GO

The graph below shows the profits made by two different companies over a four-year period. Use the graph to answer questions 18 through 20.

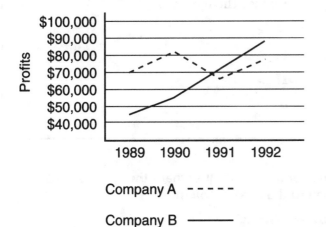

Company A - - - - -

Company B ——

18 In which year did the profits of Company A first fall below those of Company B?

   F 1992
   G 1989
   H 1990
   J 1991

19 How much did Company A earn during the year it had its highest profits?

   A $82,000
   B $87,000
   C $67,000
   D $70,000

20 In 1989, Company B spent 10% of its profits on research and development. Company A spent 5% of its profits in the same year on research and development. How much money did Company B spend?

   F $5500
   G $44,000
   H $4500
   J $7500

21 Suppose you knew the monthly cost of cable television, the number of channels you can receive, and the number of people in a family. Which of these questions could you answer?

   A The amount of time spent watching TV
   B The average cost per channel
   C How long it takes to install the cable
   D The average cost per program

Read this passage, then do numbers 22 through 24.

A bus driver began her route with an empty bus. She picked up 8 passengers at the first stop. Each passenger paid $1.50. At the next stop, 12 passengers got on. Half of them were senior citizens, so they paid only $.75. At the third stop, 5 more passengers got on the bus and 8 got off.

22 What was the total number of passengers that got on the bus?

   F 17
   G 25
   H 19
   J 33

23 What was the total amount of money the passengers paid?

   A $37.50
   B $27.50
   C $33.00
   D $33.50

24 After the third stop, how many people were on the bus?

   F 33
   G 19
   H 18
   J 17

STOP

Example   **Directions:** Find the correct answer to each measurement problem. Mark the space for your choice.

A What is the value of z in the number sentence $12 \times z = 72$?

    A 84

    B 7

    C 60

    D 6

B If $4 < c$ and $c < d$, what should replace the box in $4 \ \square \ d$?

    F <

    G –

    H >

    J =

 **Tips**

If you are sure you know which answer is correct, just mark the space for your answer and move on to the next problem.

Eliminate answer choices you know are wrong.

Practice

1 Which statement is true if n is a whole number?

    A If $n - 9 = 18$, then $9 + n = 18$.

    B If $9 + n = 18$, then $18 + 9 = n$.

    C If $9 \times n = 18$, then $18 \div n = 9$.

    D If $9 \div n = 18$, then $18 \times 9 = n$.

2 If $x > 105$ and $x < 148$, which of the following is a possible value of x?

    F 371

    G 103

    H 173

    J 137

3 Nine people go for a ride in two cars. One car holds three more people than the other. How many people are in each car?

    A 6 in one car and 3 in another

    B 5 in one car and 4 in the other

    C 8 in one car and 1 in the other

    D 2 in one car and 7 in the other

4 What point is at (5, 3)?

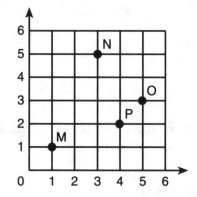

    F M

    G N

    H O

    J P

5 What is the value of z if $56 \div z = 8$?

    A 6

    B 7

    C 60

    D 45

STOP

Examples   **Directions:** Read and work each problem. Find the correct answer. Mark the space for your choice.

E1

A desk normally costs $129. It is on sale for $99. How much would you save if you bought 2 desks on sale?

A ($129 + $99) x 2 = ☐

B ($129 − $99) ÷ 2 = ☐

C ($129 − $99) x 2 = ☐

D ($129 + $99) ÷ 2 = ☐

E2

How many pints are in 5 quarts?

F 10

G 7

H 20

J 15

---

1 The highway department uses 6 gallons of paint for every 10 blocks of highway stripe. How many gallons will be needed for 250 blocks of highway stripe?

A (6 x 10) + 250 = ☐

B 250 − (10 ÷ 6) = ☐

C 250 x 10 x 6 = ☐

D (250 ÷ 10) x 6 = ☐

2 A hiker started out with 48 ounces of water. She drank 9 ounces of water after hiking 5 miles and 16 more ounces when she reached mile marker 8. How many ounces of water did she have left?

F 48 − (9 + 16) = ☐

G 48 + (9 − 16) = ☐

H (16 − 9) + 48 = ☐

J 48 + 9 + 16 = ☐

3 An electrician has 300 feet of wire. He uses 275 feet and saves the rest for another job. How many feet of wire does he have left?

A 300 + ☐ = 275

B 300 + 275 = ☐

C 300 − ☐ = 275

D ☐ = 300 + 275

4 What are the coordinates of point P ?

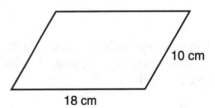

F (−3, 2)

G (2, 3)

H (5, 0)

J (−3, 3)

5 What is the perimeter of this parallelogram?

18 cm   10 cm

A 56 cm

B 28 cm

C 180 cm

D 58 cm

GO

The chart below shows how the space in a house was divided among the different rooms. Use the chart to answer numbers 6 through 8.

6 What fraction of the space in the house is the kitchen?

F $\frac{1}{5}$

G $\frac{2}{5}$

H $\frac{1}{5}$

J $\frac{1}{8}$

7 What percentage of the space in the house are the bathrooms?

A 8%

B 12.5%

C 18%

D 1.25%

8 If the total space in the house is 2000 square feet, how many square feet of space is taken up by the bedrooms?

F 300

G 310

H 600

J 60

9 Which of these shows a ray?

A ←——→

B •——•

C •——→

D ◯

10 Paul's fishing rod is 1.5 meters long. How many millimeters long is it?

F 150

G 150,000

H 15,000

J Not Given

11 What is the value of z if $14 \times z = 42$?

A 28

B 39

C 3

D 45

12 When Sandy and her father went to the supermarket, they bought $17.84 worth of food. Sandy's father paid for the food with a $20 bill. Which of these is the correct amount of change they should receive?

F 2 one-dollar bills, 1 dime, 1 nickel, and 1 penny

G 3 one-dollar bills, 1 dime, 1 nickel, and 1 penny

H 2 one-dollar bills, 1 dime, 2 nickels, and 1 penny

J Not Given

GO

13 Suppose a worker receives a raise each year except one. In that one year, the worker was paid less than the year before. Which of the graphs below show this pattern?

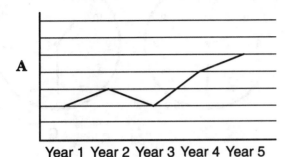

A

Year 1 Year 2 Year 3 Year 4 Year 5

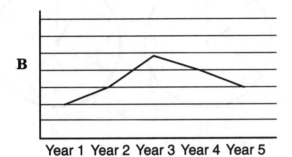

B

Year 1 Year 2 Year 3 Year 4 Year 5

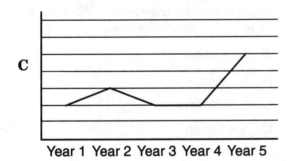

C

Year 1 Year 2 Year 3 Year 4 Year 5

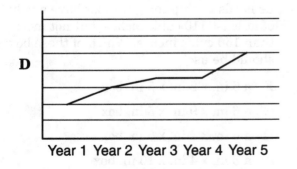

D

Year 1 Year 2 Year 3 Year 4 Year 5

Read this passage, then do numbers 14 and 15.

Harriet and Bernardo volunteered to pick up litter at a park near their home. They will work from 9:00 A.M. to 2 P.M. each Saturday.

14 If there are 4 Saturdays in a month, how many hours in all do Harriet and Bernardo work in a month?

F 35 hours

G 5 hours

H 24 hours

J Not Given

15 It usually takes one person 2 hours to fill one bag of trash at the park. How many bags of trash will Harriet and Bernardo pick up together in one day?

A 4

B 2.5

C 5

D Not Given

---

16 What is the area of the shaded shape?

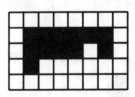

☐ = 1 square unit

F 13 square units

G 12 square units

H 9 square units

J Not Given

GO

17 About how long is the rectangle above the ruler?

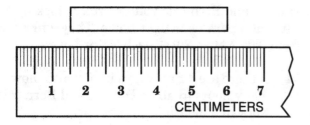

A 6 cm

B 4.5 cm

C 5.5 cm

D Not Given

18 Suppose you knew the number of pages in a book, how long it takes to read a page, and the number of words on a page. Which of these questions could you not answer?

F How many letters are in the book?

G How long does it take to read the book?

H How many words are in the book?

J How long does it take to read the number of words on one page?

19 What is the perimeter of the shaded figure below?

A 17 units

B 12 units

C 8 units

D 16 units

20 Which clock shows that the time is 2 hours and 30 minutes before midnight?

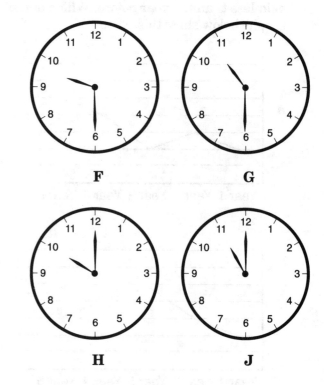

21 Four trees are 4.3 meters, 2.5 meters, 2.9 meters, and 3.3 meters tall. What is the average height of the trees?

A 4.5 meters

B 13 meters

C 3.25 meters

D Not Given

22 Louis is shipping a gift to a friend. The box he needs to ship the gift must have a volume of at least 110 cubic inches, but not more than 150 cubic inches. Which of these boxes should he use?

F a 6 in. x 2 in. x 5 in. box

G a 6 in. x 9 in. x 5 in. box

H a 6 in. x 4 in. x 5 in. box

J a 6 in. x 4 in. x 10 in. box

STOP

Name and Answer Sheet

To the Student:

These tests will give you a chance to put the tips you have learned to work.

A few last reminders…

- Be sure you understand all the directions before you begin each test. You may ask the teacher questions about the directions if you do not understand them.
- Work as quickly as you can during each test.
- When you change an answer, be sure to erase your first mark completely.

- You can guess at an answer or skip difficult items and go back to them later.
- Use the tips you have learned whenever you can.
- It is OK to be a little nervous. You may even do better.

Now that you have completed the lessons in this unit, you are on your way to scoring high!

STUDENT'S NAME		SCHOOL

LAST   FIRST   MI

TEACHER

FEMALE ◯   MALE ◯

BIRTHDATE

MONTH	DAY	YEAR
JAN ◯	⓪ ⓪	⓪
FEB ◯	① ①	①
MAR ◯	② ②	②
APR ◯	③ ③	③
MAY ◯	④	④
JUN ◯	⑤	⑤ ⑤
JUL ◯	⑥	⑥ ⑥
AUG ◯	⑦	⑦ ⑦
SEP ◯	⑧	⑧ ⑧
OCT ◯	⑨	⑨ ⑨
NOV ◯		
DEC ◯		

GRADE

⑤   ⑥   ⑦   ⑧   ⑨   ⑩

(Name grid with bubbles A–Z for each letter column)

139

PART 1   CONCEPTS

E1 Ⓐ Ⓑ Ⓒ Ⓓ	**4** Ⓕ Ⓖ Ⓗ Ⓙ	**9** Ⓐ Ⓑ Ⓒ Ⓓ	**14** Ⓕ Ⓖ Ⓗ Ⓙ	**19** Ⓐ Ⓑ Ⓒ Ⓓ	**24** Ⓕ Ⓖ Ⓗ Ⓙ
E2 Ⓕ Ⓖ Ⓗ Ⓙ	**5** Ⓐ Ⓑ Ⓒ Ⓓ	**10** Ⓕ Ⓖ Ⓗ Ⓙ	**15** Ⓐ Ⓑ Ⓒ Ⓓ	**20** Ⓕ Ⓖ Ⓗ Ⓙ	**25** Ⓐ Ⓑ Ⓒ Ⓓ
1 Ⓐ Ⓑ Ⓒ Ⓓ	**6** Ⓕ Ⓖ Ⓗ Ⓙ	**11** Ⓐ Ⓑ Ⓒ Ⓓ	**16** Ⓕ Ⓖ Ⓗ Ⓙ	**21** Ⓐ Ⓑ Ⓒ Ⓓ	
2 Ⓕ Ⓖ Ⓗ Ⓙ	**7** Ⓐ Ⓑ Ⓒ Ⓓ	**12** Ⓕ Ⓖ Ⓗ Ⓙ	**17** Ⓐ Ⓑ Ⓒ Ⓓ	**22** Ⓕ Ⓖ Ⓗ Ⓙ	
3 Ⓐ Ⓑ Ⓒ Ⓓ	**8** Ⓕ Ⓖ Ⓗ Ⓙ	**13** Ⓐ Ⓑ Ⓒ Ⓓ	**18** Ⓕ Ⓖ Ⓗ Ⓙ	**23** Ⓐ Ⓑ Ⓒ Ⓓ	

PART 2   COMPUTATION

E1 Ⓐ Ⓑ Ⓒ Ⓓ Ⓔ	**3** Ⓐ Ⓑ Ⓒ Ⓓ Ⓔ	**7** Ⓐ Ⓑ Ⓒ Ⓓ Ⓔ	**11** Ⓐ Ⓑ Ⓒ Ⓓ Ⓔ	**15** Ⓐ Ⓑ Ⓒ Ⓓ Ⓔ	**19** Ⓐ Ⓑ Ⓒ Ⓓ Ⓔ
E2 Ⓕ Ⓖ Ⓗ Ⓙ Ⓚ	**4** Ⓕ Ⓖ Ⓗ Ⓙ Ⓚ	**8** Ⓕ Ⓖ Ⓗ Ⓙ Ⓚ	**12** Ⓕ Ⓖ Ⓗ Ⓙ Ⓚ	**16** Ⓕ Ⓖ Ⓗ Ⓙ Ⓚ	**20** Ⓕ Ⓖ Ⓗ Ⓙ Ⓚ
1 Ⓐ Ⓑ Ⓒ Ⓓ Ⓔ	**5** Ⓐ Ⓑ Ⓒ Ⓓ Ⓔ	**9** Ⓐ Ⓑ Ⓒ Ⓓ Ⓔ	**13** Ⓐ Ⓑ Ⓒ Ⓓ Ⓔ	**17** Ⓐ Ⓑ Ⓒ Ⓓ Ⓔ	**21** Ⓐ Ⓑ Ⓒ Ⓓ Ⓔ
2 Ⓕ Ⓖ Ⓗ Ⓙ Ⓚ	**6** Ⓕ Ⓖ Ⓗ Ⓙ Ⓚ	**10** Ⓕ Ⓖ Ⓗ Ⓙ Ⓚ	**14** Ⓕ Ⓖ Ⓗ Ⓙ Ⓚ	**18** Ⓕ Ⓖ Ⓗ Ⓙ Ⓚ	**22** Ⓕ Ⓖ Ⓗ Ⓙ Ⓚ

PART 3   APPLICATIONS

E1 Ⓐ Ⓑ Ⓒ Ⓓ	**4** Ⓕ Ⓖ Ⓗ Ⓙ	**9** Ⓐ Ⓑ Ⓒ Ⓓ	**14** Ⓕ Ⓖ Ⓗ Ⓙ	**19** Ⓐ Ⓑ Ⓒ Ⓓ	**22** Ⓕ Ⓖ Ⓗ Ⓙ
E2 Ⓕ Ⓖ Ⓗ Ⓙ	**5** Ⓐ Ⓑ Ⓒ Ⓓ	**10** Ⓕ Ⓖ Ⓗ Ⓙ	**15** Ⓐ Ⓑ Ⓒ Ⓓ	**20** Ⓕ Ⓖ Ⓗ Ⓙ	**23** Ⓐ Ⓑ Ⓒ Ⓓ
1 Ⓐ Ⓑ Ⓒ Ⓓ	**6** Ⓕ Ⓖ Ⓗ Ⓙ	**11** Ⓐ Ⓑ Ⓒ Ⓓ	**16** Ⓕ Ⓖ Ⓗ Ⓙ	**21** Ⓐ Ⓑ Ⓒ Ⓓ	**24** Ⓕ Ⓖ Ⓗ Ⓙ
2 Ⓕ Ⓖ Ⓗ Ⓙ	**7** Ⓐ Ⓑ Ⓒ Ⓓ	**12** Ⓕ Ⓖ Ⓗ Ⓙ	**17** Ⓐ Ⓑ Ⓒ Ⓓ		
3 Ⓐ Ⓑ Ⓒ Ⓓ	**8** Ⓕ Ⓖ Ⓗ Ⓙ	**13** Ⓐ Ⓑ Ⓒ Ⓓ	**18** Ⓕ Ⓖ Ⓗ Ⓙ		

UNIT 4   TEST PRACTICE

Examples   **Directions:** Read and work each problem. Find the correct answer. Mark the space for your choice.

E1

$$\frac{8}{10,000} =$$

A 8.0000

B 0.0800

C 0.8000

D 0.0008

E2

Which two numbers are <u>both</u> factors of 56?

F 16, 6

G 7, 8

H 9, 6

J 5, 6

---

1 Which figure has the same shaded area as figure A?

A

A

B

C

D

2 Which number is ten thousand more than 497,205?

F   498,205

G   597,205

H   507,205

J   10,497,205

3 What is another name for 30?

A (4 + 2) x 5

B (20 x 2) ÷ 3

C 3 x (10 x 10)

D 3 x (15 ÷ 4)

4 Point P is closest in value to —

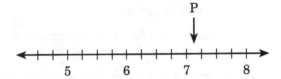

F 8.7

G 7.275

H 7.125

J 6.7

5 Which fraction is another name for $\frac{1}{5}$?

A $\frac{4}{90}$

B $\frac{5}{30}$

C $\frac{6}{65}$

D $\frac{9}{45}$

6 What number is missing from the pattern shown below?

| 9, 10, 13, 18, ___ , 34, 45 |

F 23

G 25

H 26

J 24

141

GO

7 Which of these does not have the same value as the others?

  A $\frac{21}{3}$

  B $\sqrt{49}$

  C 0.7

  D 14 x 0.5

8 Which of these statements is true about the number 190,427?

  F It has a 9 in the thousands place and a 2 in the tens place.

  G It has a 0 in the thousands place and a 2 in the tens place.

  H It has a 1 in the ten thousands place and a 4 in the hundreds place.

  J It has a 9 in the ten thousands place and a 4 in the thousands place.

9 How many of the fractions in the box are greater than $\frac{2}{3}$?

$$\frac{2}{5} \quad \frac{3}{4} \quad \frac{5}{8} \quad \frac{6}{7} \quad \frac{4}{9} \quad \frac{8}{19}$$

  A 2

  B 1

  C 5

  D 4

10 What should replace the box in the number sentence below?

$$(8 \times \square) - 6 = 18$$

  F 2

  G 3

  H 10

  J 4

11 Which statement is true about the number sentence $983 \div 10 = \square$?

  A $\square$ is more than 100.

  B $\square$ is less than 90.

  C $\square$ is less than 100.

  D $\square$ is more than 1000.

12 What should replace the $\square$ in the number sentence below?

$$3 \times 6 = (3 \times 4) + (3 \times \square)$$

  F 2

  G 3

  H 1

  J 6

13 Which fraction is in its simplest form?

  A $\frac{3}{9}$

  B $\frac{2}{10}$

  C $\frac{3}{5}$

  D $\frac{10}{12}$

14 Which is a multiple of 14?

  F 54

  G 7

  H 56

  J 38

15 If this number pattern continues, what number would come next in the pattern?

$$5, 12, 9, 17, 13, \_\_\_$$

  A 17

  B 21

  C 22

  D 20

16 Which of these is the expanded numeral for 43,028?

   F 430 + 28

   G 43,000 + 200 + 80

   H 4300 + 200 + 8

   J 43,000 + 20 + 8

17 Which digit means tens of thousands in the numeral 397,108?

   A 7

   B 3

   C 9

   D 1

18 Which of these is 0.385 rounded to the nearest tenth?

   F 0.4

   G 0.3

   H 0.310

   J 0.410

19 $\sqrt{100}$

   A 11

   B 10

   C 25

   D 9

20 Which is the least whole number that makes the number sentence below true?

$$5 \times \square < 60$$

   F 12

   G 11

   H 14

   J 20

21 Which of these is another name for $\frac{8}{3}$?

   A 3

   B $1\frac{2}{3}$

   C $2\frac{3}{8}$

   D $2\frac{2}{3}$

22 Which of these is a prime number?

   F 23

   G 21

   H 12

   J 32

23 Which period is underlined in the numeral 387,103,254?

   A hundred millions

   B ten thousands

   C millions

   D hundred thousands

24 If you are estimating the sum of 287 plus 419 by rounding to the nearest ten and then to the nearest hundred, what will be the estimated sums?

   F 710 and 700

   G 690 and 700

   H 710 and 800

   J 700 and 800

25 Suppose you had 5 apples, 8 oranges, and 2 bananas. What fraction of the fruit would the apples be?

   A $\frac{5}{10}$

   B $\frac{1}{5}$

   C $\frac{1}{15}$

   D $\frac{1}{3}$

STOP

Examples   **Directions:** Find the correct answer to each problem. Mark the space for your choice.

E1

$300 \overline{)9000}$

A   3
B   3000
C   30
D   300
E   None of these

E2

$4.6 + .2 = \square$

F   48
G   6.6
H   4.26
J   4.62
K   None of these

1

$3200 + 5138 + 864 =$

A   8212
B   8202
C   9212
D   9202
E   None of these

6

$\begin{array}{r} 63.64 \\ -\ 3.2 \\ \hline \end{array}$

F   60.62
G   63.32
H   31.64
J   60.44
K   None of these

2

$\begin{array}{r} 5000 \\ \times\ 90 \\ \hline \end{array}$

F   59,000
G   45,000
H   450
J   4500
K   None of these

7

$7 \overline{)5016}$

A   717
B   716 R4
C   718
D   717 R6
E   None of these

3

$\begin{array}{r} 7142 \\ -\ 5086 \\ \hline \end{array}$

A   2056
B   2144
C   1056
D   2044
E   None of these

8

$\begin{array}{r} 619 \\ \times\ 509 \\ \hline \end{array}$

F   305,071
G   315,171
H   315,179
J   31,571
K   None of these

4

$782 \div 46 =$

F   16 R6
G   16
H   17
J   17 R4
K   None of these

9

$\frac{3}{4} - \frac{1}{8} = \square$

A $\frac{2}{4}$
B $\frac{2}{8}$
C $\frac{3}{5}$
D $\frac{5}{8}$
E   None of these

5

$\frac{3}{4} \times \frac{4}{7} =$

A $\frac{7}{11}$
B $\frac{3}{7}$
C $\frac{1}{28}$
D $\frac{1}{3}$
E   None of these

10

$335 \overline{)990}$

F   3 R5
G   3
H   2 R320
J   2 R65
K   None of these

GO

11

$\frac{4}{7} \times \frac{1}{3} = \square$

A $\frac{5}{21}$

B 7

C $\frac{4}{37}$

D $\frac{2}{5}$

E None of these

12

143 x 5 =

F 615

G 715

H 751

J 148

K None of these

13

2.7 + .4 + 8 =

A 14.7

B 10.1

C 3.9

D 11.1

E None of these

14

23$\overline{)207}$

F 10 R7

G 11 R4

H 9

J 8

K None of these

15

$\frac{6}{9}$
$+ \frac{7}{9}$

A $1\frac{4}{9}$

B 1

C $1\frac{1}{9}$

D 2

E None of these

16

$\frac{1}{6} + \frac{3}{4} = \square$

F $1\frac{1}{6}$

G $1\frac{3}{24}$

H $\frac{11}{12}$

J $\frac{11}{24}$

K None of these

17

12$\overline{)91.2}$

A 7.06

B 7.6

C 8.2

D 8.04

E None of these

18

8053
$-$ 210

F 8263

G 7863

H 7743

J 7833

K None of these

19

4942
x   4

A 19,368

B 16,768

C 4246

D 19,768

E None of these

20

20.4 ÷ 5 = $\square$

F 4.45

G 15.4

H 4.08

J 4.8

K None of these

21

$4\frac{2}{3}$
$+ 8\frac{1}{12}$

A $12\frac{3}{4}$

B $12\frac{7}{12}$

C 13

D $12\frac{5}{6}$

E None of these

22   (2 x 4) + (7 x 4) ÷ 9 =

F 6 R4

G 4

H 9 R7

J 3

K None of these

STOP

Examples   Directions: Read and work each problem. Find the correct answer. Mark the space for your choice.

E1

If 24 students each bring 5 cans of food to school for the homeless, how many cans do they bring in all?

A 24 + 5 = ☐

B 24 − 5 = ☐

C 24 x 5 = ☐

D 24 ÷ 5 = ☐

E2

How much change will you receive from $2.00 if you buy a pencil for $.19 and a pen for $.79?

F $1.21

G $1.81

H $1.01

J Not Given

---

1 What is the total attendance at a picnic if there are 56 girls and 48 boys?

A 56 + 48 = ☐

B 56 − 48 = ☐

C 56 x 48 = ☐

D 56 ÷ 48 = ☐

2 A carpenter has 10 pieces of wood that are each 8 feet long. She has to cut 2 feet from each piece of wood because of water damage. How much good wood does she have left?

F (8 + 2) x 10 = ☐

G (10 − 2) x 8 = ☐

H (10 x 8) − 2 = ☐

J (8 − 2) x 10 = ☐

3 A barrel is 36 inches from top to bottom. The water in the barrel is $12\frac{1}{2}$ inches deep. How much space is there from the surface of the water to the top of the barrel?

A ☐ = $36 \div 12\frac{1}{2}$

B ☐ = $36 \times 12\frac{1}{2}$

C ☐ = $36 - 12\frac{1}{2}$

D ☐ = $36 + 12\frac{1}{2}$

4 Clark lives in a building that is 5 stories tall. About how tall is the building?

F 100 feet

G 50 feet

H 5000 feet

J 10 feet

5 What is the perimeter of this rectangle?

6 cm

27 cm

A 33 cm

B 60 cm

C 66 cm

D Not Given

6 Which of these statements is correct?

F 9 quarters is worth more than 12 dimes.

G 12 dimes is worth more than 50 nickels.

H 50 nickels is worth less than 9 quarters.

J 50 nickels is worth less than 12 dimes.

7 If x + 9 = 27, then x =

A 3

B 16

C 36

D 18

GO >

8 In which of these drawings is $\overline{CD}$ perpendicular to $\overline{GH}$?

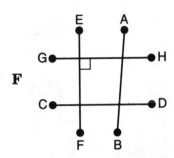

F

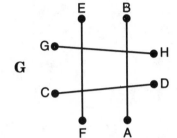

G

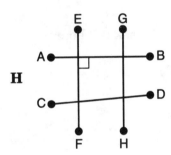

H

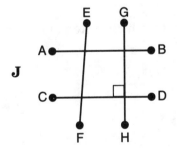

J

9 Suppose you wrote the word YESTERDAY on a strip of paper and cut the paper into pieces with just one letter on each piece. If you put the pieces into a bag and pulled one piece out without looking at it, what is the probability you would pick out the letter Y?

   A 1 out of 9

   B 2 out of 9

   C 1 out of 2

   D 2 out of 7

The graph below shows the number of school-age children in five different towns in two different years. Use the graph to answer questions 10 through 12.

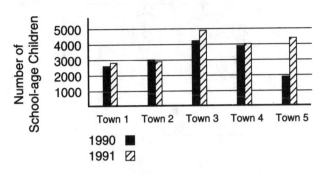

10 In which town were there about 2800 school-age children in 1991?

   F Town 3

   G Town 4

   H Town 5

   J Not Given

11 In which town did the number of school-age children increase by more than 2000?

   A Town 2

   B Town 5

   C Town 1

   D Not Given

12 In Town 2 during 1990 there were three times as many adults as there were school-age children. During the same year, there were half as many pre-school children as school-age children. Based on this information, which of these questions would you be able to answer?

   F What was the total population of Town 2 in 1990?

   G How many pre-school children were in Town 2 in 1991?

   H How many adults were in Town 2 in 1991?

   J How many children in Town 2 began school in 1991?

GO

13 What is the perimeter of the larger rectangle below?

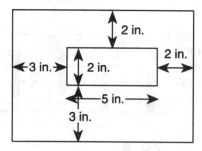

A 28 in.

B 34 in.

C 70 in.

D 17 in.

Read this passage, then answer questions 14 and 15.

The base of Sandy Mountain is 5400 feet above sea level. The top of the mountain is 10,700 feet above sea level. A trail runs from the base of the mountain to the top. The trail is 8 miles long, and it takes about 5 hours to hike from the base of the mountain to the top.

14 What is the vertical distance from the base of the mountain to the top?

F 5300 feet

G 6300 feet

H 10,700 feet

J 4700 feet

15 Carol and her friends are hiking from the base of the mountain to the top. They start at 9:00 A.M. and take a break at 11:00 A.M. for lunch. How far have they hiked?

A 5.6 miles

B 4.8 miles

C 2.5 miles

D 3.2 miles

16 What is the area of the shaded figure below?

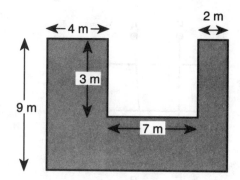

F 117 m²

G 21 m²

H 96 m²

J 25 m²

17 What fraction of 1 week is 8 hours?

A $\frac{1}{21}$

B $\frac{1}{7}$

C $\frac{1}{24}$

D $\frac{1}{8}$

18 If $10 < k$ and $k < l$, which statement below is true?

F $10 + l = k$

G $10 = l$

H $10 > l$

J $10 < l$

19 Gina and Rob are helping their parents pick apples. They work for 7 hours and each pick 19 bags full of apples. If it takes 12 bags of apples to fill 1 box, how many boxes of apples will they fill completely?

A 5

B 4

C 3

D 2

GO

20 Which point is at (4, –3) ?

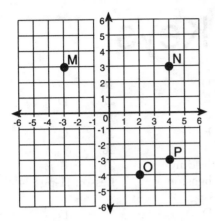

F M

G N

H O

J P

21 Which pair of shapes is congruent?

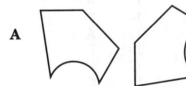

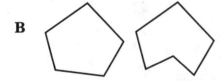

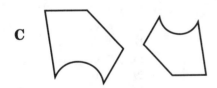

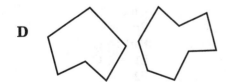

22 100 inches is —

F more than 3 yards

G between 8 and 9 feet

H exactly 10 feet

J less than 2 yards

23 A truck driver starts out at 8:30 A.M. and drives for 5 hours before stopping for lunch. He spends 45 minutes at lunch and then continues his trip. What time did he stop for lunch?

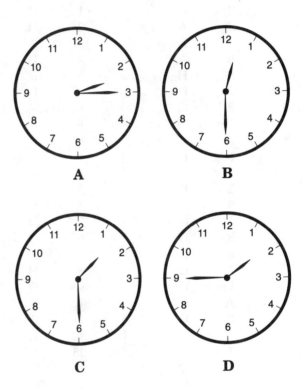

24 The Perez family is planning next year's vacation. They want to save $20 each week for 52 weeks. The three children in the family will each give $1 a week, Mrs. Perez will give $10, and Mr. Perez will give the rest. How much money will they have for vacation?

F $72

G $2600

H $140

J $1040

STOP

Answer Keys

Reading
Unit 1,
Vocabulary
Lesson 1-pg.13

A	D
B	F
1	C
2	J
3	A
4	F
5	A
6	H
7	D
8	G

Lesson 2-pg.14

A	C
B	J
1	B
2	F
3	D
4	G
5	D
6	F
7	C

Lesson 3-pg.15

A	C
B	G
1	C
2	F
3	D
4	G
5	B
6	H
7	A
8	J

Lesson 4-pg.16

A	C
B	G
1	D
2	F
3	A
4	J
5	D

Lesson 5-pg.17

A	A
B	J

1	C
2	G
3	D
4	F
5	D
6	G

Lesson 6-pg.18

A	C
B	G
1	D
2	H
3	A
4	H
5	B
6	F

Lesson 7-pgs.19-22

E1	D
E2	F
1	C
2	F
3	D
4	H
5	D
6	G
7	A
8	H
9	D
10	F
11	B
12	H
13	D
14	J
15	C
16	G
17	D
18	F
19	A
20	H
21	B
22	F
23	C
24	F
25	C
26	H
27	A
28	H
29	A
30	G

31	D
32	J
33	C
34	F
35	B

Unit 2, Reading
Comprehension
Lesson 8-pg.23

A	D
1	C
2	F
3	D
4	G

Lesson 9-pgs.24-27

A	A
1	D
2	H
3	C
4	F
5	B
6	J
7	B
8	H
9	D
10	H
11	A
12	G
13	B
14	H
15	A
16	J

Lesson 10-pgs.28-33

A	C
1	A
2	F
3	D
4	H
5	D
6	F
7	B
8	H
9	A
10	J
11	C
12	F
13	C
14	F
15	B

16	G
17	D
18	F
19	C
20	J
21	B

Lesson 11-pgs.34-42

A	B
1	D
2	G
3	C
4	F
5	A
6	H
7	B
8	H
9	D
10	J
11	A
12	H
13	B
14	F
15	A
16	J
17	C
18	G
19	A
20	J
21	D
22	J
23	D
24	F
25	C
26	G
27	A
28	G
29	B
30	J

Unit 3, Test
Practice
Part 1-pgs.45-48

E1	C
E2	J
1	B
2	J
3	D
4	G
5	D

6 H
7 D
8 G
9 D
10 F
11 B
12 J
13 C
14 F
15 B
16 F
17 D
18 H
19 B
20 H
21 B
22 F
23 D
24 G
25 B
26 J
27 C
28 G
29 A
30 H
31 A
32 F
33 B
34 J
35 C

Test Practice
Part 2-pgs.49-57
A D
1 A
2 J
3 B
4 H
5 B
6 H
7 D
8 F
9 D
10 F
11 C
12 F
13 B
14 H
15 D
16 F
17 C
18 G
19 D
20 F

21 C
22 J
23 D
24 G
25 B
26 G
27 D
28 J
29 A
30 G
31 C
32 F
33 D
34 G
35 C

Language
Unit 1, Language
Mechanics
Lesson 1-pgs.59-60
A C
B J
1 C
2 J
3 A
4 G
5 B
6 H
7 C
8 G
9 D
10 H
11 A
12 F
13 A
14 H
15 D
16 G

Lesson 2-pgs.61-63
A B
B J
1 D
2 F
3 B
4 H
5 A
6 J
7 D
8 H
9 A
10 G
11 C
12 F
13 D
14 G

15 D
16 F
17 A
18 H
19 B
20 J

Lesson 3-pgs.64-67
E1 A
1 D
2 H
3 A
4 G
5 D
6 F
7 B
8 H
9 A
10 J
11 B
12 H
13 A
14 H
15 A
16 J
17 B
18 G
19 C
20 J
21 A
22 G
23 A
24 H
25 D
26 G
27 A
28 H
29 B

Unit 2, Language
Expression
Lesson 4-pgs.68-70
A A
B J
1 C
2 H
3 A
4 G
5 D
6 H
7 C
8 G
9 D
10 F
11 B
12 F

13 D
14 G
15 C
16 F
17 C
18 F
19 B
20 G

Lesson 5-pgs.71-73
A B
B H
C A
1 B
2 G
3 C
4 G
5 C
6 G
7 C
8 J
9 A
10 H
11 B
12 F
13 C
14 J
15 B

Lesson 6-pgs.74-77
A D
1 C
2 F
3 C
4 F
5 B
6 J
7 C
8 G
9 D
10 F
11 B
12 J
13 A
14 H

Lesson 7-pgs.78-81
E1 C
1 B
2 F
3 D
4 H
5 B
6 F
7 C
8 H

9	B
10	J
11	B
12	F
13	A
14	J
15	B
16	H
17	B
18	J
19	C
20	F

Unit 3, Spelling
Lesson 8-pgs.82-83

A	B
B	H
1	B
2	H
3	D
4	G
5	A
6	G
7	D
8	F
9	A
10	K
11	D
12	H
13	B
14	H
15	A
16	J
17	B
18	G

Lesson 9-pgs.84-85

E1	D
E2	F
1	A
2	G
3	C
4	H
5	A
6	J
7	B
8	H
9	B
10	J
11	B
12	H
13	A
14	H
15	D
16	F

17	A
18	J
19	B
20	F

Unit 4, Study Skills
Lesson 10-pgs.86-87

A	C
1	A
2	J
3	C
4	H
5	D
6	G
7	B
8	H
9	A
10	J
11	C
12	J
13	D

Lesson 11-pgs.88-90

E1	A
E2	H
1	B
2	F
3	D
4	F
5	A
6	J
7	C
8	G
9	C
10	J
11	A
12	F
13	C
14	H
15	A
16	J
17	B
18	H

Unit 5, Test Practice
Part 1-pgs.93-95

E1	D
1	B
2	F
3	B
4	J
5	D
6	F
7	C

8	G
9	C
10	H
11	D
12	G
13	A
14	F
15	C
16	J
17	C
18	J
19	B
20	F
21	C

Test Practice
Part 2-pgs.96-99

E1	C
1	C
2	G
3	B
4	G
5	D
6	G
7	C
8	F
9	C
10	G
11	B
12	H
13	C
14	F
15	D
16	G
17	B
18	J
19	D
20	H

Test Practice
Part 3-pgs.100-101

E1	B
E2	H
1	B
2	J
3	A
4	G
5	C
6	G
7	D
8	F
9	C
10	G
11	E
12	H
13	A

14	J
15	B
16	H
17	B
18	F
19	D
20	H

Test Practice
Part 4-pgs.102-103

E1	B
1	D
2	H
3	A
4	G
5	C
6	G
7	A
8	F
9	D
10	H

Math
Unit 1, Concepts
Lesson 1-pgs.105-106

A	D
B	G
1	D
2	F
3	B
4	H
5	C
6	G
7	A
8	G
9	D
10	H
11	D
12	H
13	D
14	F
15	B
16	J

Lesson 2-pgs.107-108

A	B
B	J
1	C
2	F
3	D
4	G
5	C
6	H
7	D
8	F
9	B
10	H

11	A
12	J
13	B
14	H
15	B

Lesson 3-pgs.109-110

A	B
B	F
1	A
2	H
3	B
4	J
5	B
6	J
7	B
8	F
9	C
10	J
11	B

Lesson 4-pgs.111-112

A	C
1	D
2	H
3	D
4	G
5	A
6	J
7	C
8	F
9	B
10	F
11	D
12	G
13	B

Lesson 5-pgs.113-114

E1	C
E2	F
1	A
2	G
3	B
4	J
5	C
6	J
7	C
8	H
9	B
10	J
11	A
12	F
13	C
14	J
15	B

Unit 2, Computation

Lesson 6-pgs.115-116

A	D
B	K
1	C
2	K
3	A
4	H
5	B
6	G
7	D
8	G
9	D
10	F
11	C
12	G
13	E
14	F
15	C
16	J
17	E
18	H

Lesson 7-pgs.117-118

A	A
B	K
1	E
2	J
3	B
4	J
5	D
6	K
7	C
8	F
9	D
10	K
11	A
12	H
13	D
14	H
15	A
16	G
17	E
18	H
19	D

Lesson 8-pgs.119-120

A	B
B	K
1	C
2	H
3	A
4	K
5	B
6	H
7	B
8	J
9	D
10	K
11	C
12	F
13	B
14	K
15	A
16	J
17	B
18	H
19	A

Lesson 9-pgs.121-122

A	D
B	H
1	D
2	G
3	C
4	F
5	A
6	J
7	C
8	G
9	C
10	G
11	A
12	J
13	B
14	F
15	A
16	G
17	D
18	H
19	A
20	H

Unit 3, Applications

Lesson 10-pgs.123-124

E1	D
E2	K
1	C
2	K
3	B
4	H
5	B
6	F
7	C
8	J
9	D
10	H
11	A
12	G
13	D
14	K
15	C
16	J
17	C
18	F
19	B
20	K
21	B
22	G

Lesson 11-pgs.125-127

A	B
1	A
2	H
3	D
4	G
5	D
6	G
7	C
8	F
9	C
10	G
11	D
12	F
13	C
14	J
15	B
16	J
17	A

Lesson 12-pgs.128-129

A	B
1	D
2	F
3	B
4	H
5	D
6	F
7	C
8	G
9	A
10	G
11	D
12	H

Lesson 13-pgs.130-133

A	B
B	J
1	C
2	F
3	D
4	G

5	A	15	C	3	A	19	C
6	G	16	G	4	H	20	J
7	D	17	B	5	B	21	A
8	J	18	F	6	J	22	G
9	A	19	D	7	B	23	C
10	H	20	F	8	K	24	J
11	D	21	C	9	D		
12	H	22	H	10	H		
13	D	**Unit 4, Test Practice**		11	E		
14	F	**Part 1-pgs. 141-143**		12	G		
15	B	E1	D	13	D		
16	H	E2	G	14	H		
17	A	1	B	15	A		
18	J	2	H	16	H		
19	A	3	A	17	B		
20	H	4	H	18	K		
21	B	5	D	19	D		
22	G	6	G	20	H		
23	C	7	C	21	A		
24	J	8	G	22	G		
Lesson 14-pg. 134		9	A	**Test Practice**			
A	D	10	G	**Part 3-pgs. 146-149**			
B	F	11	C	E1	C		
1	C	12	F	E2	J		
2	J	13	C	1	A		
3	A	14	H	2	J		
4	H	15	C	3	C		
5	B	16	J	4	G		
Lesson 15-pgs. 135-138		17	C	5	C		
E1	C	18	F	6	F		
E2	F	19	B	7	D		
1	D	20	G	8	J		
2	F	21	D	9	B		
3	C	22	F	10	J		
4	J	23	C	11	B		
5	A	24	F	12	F		
6	J	25	D	13	B		
7	B	**Test Practice**		14	F		
8	H	**Part 2-pgs. 144-145**		15	D		
9	C	E1	C	16	H		
10	J	E2	K	17	A		
11	C	1	D	18	J		
12	F	2	K				
13	A						
14	J						

Reading Progress Chart

Circle your score for each lesson. Connect your scores to see how well you are doing.

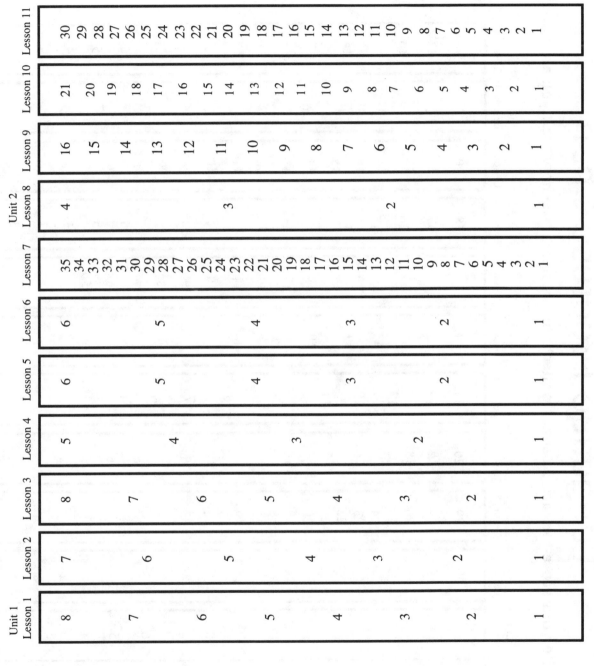

155

Language Progress Chart

Circle your score for each lesson. Connect your scores to see how well you are doing.

Unit 1			Unit 2			Unit 3			Unit 4	
Lesson 1	Lesson 2	Lesson 3	Lesson 4	Lesson 5	Lesson 6	Lesson 7	Lesson 8	Lesson 9	Lesson 10	Lesson 11
16	20	29	20	15	14	20	18	20	13	18
15	19	28	19	14	13	19	17	19	12	17
14	18	27	18	13	12	18	16	18	11	16
13	17	26	17	12	11	17	15	17	10	15
12	16	25	16	11	10	16	14	16	9	14
11	15	24	15	10	9	15	13	15	8	13
10	14	23	14	9	8	14	12	14	7	12
9	13	22	13	8	7	13	11	13	6	11
8	12	21	12	7	6	12	10	12	5	10
7	11	20	11	6	5	11	9	11	4	9
6	10	19	10	5	4	10	8	10	3	8
5	9	18	9	4	3	9	7	9	2	7
4	8	17	8	3	2	8	6	8	1	6
3	7	16	7	2	1	7	5	7		5
2	6	15	6	1		6	4	6		4
1	5	14	5			5	3	5		3
	4	13	4			4	2	4		2
	3	12	3			3	1	3		1
	2	11	2			2		2		
	1	10	1			1		1		
		9								
		8								
		7								
		6								
		5								
		4								
		3								
		2								
		1								

Math Progress Chart

Circle your score for each lesson. Connect your scores to see how well you are doing.

Unit 1

- Lesson 1: 16, 15, 14, 13, 12, 11, 10, 9, 8, 7, 6, 5, 4, 3, 2, 1
- Lesson 2: 15, 14, 13, 12, 11, 10, 9, 8, 7, 6, 5, 4, 3, 2, 1
- Lesson 3: 11, 10, 9, 8, 7, 6, 5, 4, 3, 2, 1
- Lesson 4: 13, 12, 11, 10, 9, 8, 7, 6, 5, 4, 3, 2, 1
- Lesson 5: 15, 14, 13, 12, 11, 10, 9, 8, 7, 6, 5, 4, 3, 2, 1

Unit 2

- Lesson 6: 18, 17, 16, 15, 14, 13, 12, 11, 10, 9, 8, 7, 6, 5, 4, 3, 2, 1
- Lesson 7: 19, 18, 17, 16, 15, 14, 13, 12, 11, 10, 9, 8, 7, 6, 5, 4, 3, 2, 1
- Lesson 8: 19, 18, 17, 16, 15, 14, 13, 12, 11, 10, 9, 8, 7, 6, 5, 4, 3, 2, 1
- Lesson 9: 20, 19, 18, 17, 16, 15, 14, 13, 12, 11, 10, 9, 8, 7, 6, 5, 4, 3, 2, 1
- Lesson 10: 22, 21, 20, 19, 18, 17, 16, 15, 14, 13, 12, 11, 10, 9, 8, 7, 6, 5, 4, 3, 2, 1

Unit 3

- Lesson 11: 17, 16, 15, 14, 13, 12, 11, 10, 9, 8, 7, 6, 5, 4, 3, 2, 1
- Lesson 12: 12, 11, 10, 9, 8, 7, 6, 5, 4, 3, 2, 1
- Lesson 13: 24, 23, 22, 21, 20, 19, 18, 17, 16, 15, 14, 13, 12, 11, 10, 9, 8, 7, 6, 5, 4, 3, 2, 1
- Lesson 14: 5, 4, 3, 2, 1
- Lesson 15: 22, 21, 20, 19, 18, 17, 16, 15, 14, 13, 12, 11, 10, 9, 8, 7, 6, 5, 4, 3, 2, 1